Air To Air
Mustangs & Corsairs

Creative Director: Deana Torgerson

Copy Editor: Ed Parrish

Copy Proofing: Elizabeth Charlsen

Creative Consultant: Gail Bowen

Technical Consultant: Tom Jenkins

Design Consultant: Tony Blake

Printed and bound in Singapore by:
Dai Nippon Printing Co., Ltd.
For printing information contact:
Carey Dougherty or
Makoto Tamayori
DNP America, Inc.
335 Madison Avenue
New York, NY 10017
Tel: (212)503-1060
Fax: (212)286-1505

Library of Congress Control Number: 2007934027

ISBN 978-0-9665095-8-8

Stock photography for use in advertising and promotional materials available by written permission only. For availability and pricing, contact:
Paul Bowen Photography Inc.
(316)263-5537

To purchase a book directly or
obtain pricing information for
corporate quantity orders:
1(800)697-2580

WWW.AIRTOAIR.NET

Published and Distributed by:
NORTH SHORE PRESS
2300 E. Douglas
Wichita, KS 67214 USA

NORTH
SHORE
PRESS

AIR TO AIR
MUSTANGS & CORSAIRS

Photography By Paul Bowen

FOREWORD BY KERMIT WEEKS

I'd like to thank my friend, Kermit Weeks, for providing this very personal and heartfelt foreword for *Air To Air Volume IV*. He's an incredible person, and as you read these pages you'll understand why.

Kermit became interested in aviation at age 13 when he heard the song, *Snoopy and the Red Baron* by The Royal Guardsmen. It sparked his interest in aircraft, history, and the experience of flight. Combined with a fascination for building and creating things, he bought a set of plans for a Der Jaeger, a modern homebuilt fashioned to look like a WWI German fighter. He built most of his first flyable airplane at age 17 while he was still in high school. He learned how to fly in high school as well and soloed at age 17 with only six and a half hours of training. Going away to college put a dent in the time he could devote to the project; but four years later, he test flew it at age 21.

Kermit didn't grow up with money. In fact, his dream profession in high school was to become a Crop Duster! Oil royalties from his grandfather's good fortune came in his mid-twenties, and he only then realized his financial future held the wherewithal to pursue his dreams.

Kermit indulged his passion for aerobatic flying, first with a Pitts S-2A, and then with an aircraft he designed and built, the *Weeks Special*. Flying it, he became a member of the U.S. Aerobatic Team at age 24. He later designed and built another big-engine biplane, the *Weeks Solution*. During his career he placed in the top three overall five times, won 20 medals at the World Aerobatic Championships, and was twice U.S. National Aerobatic Champion.

In 1979, Kermit started collecting antique aircraft and soon began the *Weeks Air Museum* in Miami to share his passion. He bought his first vintage aircraft, an AT-6 Texan, in anticipation of getting his second, a P-51 Mustang. Over the years, his collection grew and has now become the largest private collection of vintage aircraft, with over 140 aircraft. Rivaling some national museums, it includes an example of every American fighter from World War II, the world's largest collection of privately owned World War I airplanes, and many rare, one-of-a-kind examples including a 1944 Short Sunderland, the world's only four-engine passenger flying boat. Kermit has enough projects for several lifetimes but doesn't collect anything he doesn't intend to fly one day.

Kermit began showcasing what would become the world's largest private aircraft collection at the *Weeks Air Museum* in Miami in 1985. After Hurricane Andrew destroyed that facility and damaged most of his airplanes in 1992, he began building a site in Central Florida. The *Fantasy of Flight* attraction opened in 1995. This attraction is more exciting than a museum and more cerebral than an amusement park, and is the first step in Kermit's vision for creating a destination called *Orlampa*, which he intends to become the focal point on the planet for unleashing human potential.

Kermit's plans for expanding *Fantasy of Flight* include displaying period aircraft in period facilities: Early Flight, a World War I airfield with opposing sides, a Golden Age area and a World War II airfield. Kermit has made it known he is no longer in the museum business. Instead he intends to combine the great stories of aviation history and his aircraft as a means to an ends – to deliver the Human Experience through entertainment in a way to help people self-discover their own reality. Kermit is never one to think small, so we will be keeping an eye on his progress!

On a personal note, when you shake hands with Kermit, you'll shake a tough, callused hand, one that not only flies these beauties but also helps keep them running. Truly a renaissance man, he writes songs and books and also plays music including banjo, fiddle, guitar, and piano.

Kermit Weeks is an aviator's aviator. He's a creator and a visionary and he plans to use man's fascination with flight to help humanity take the next step on its Journey.

I'm proud to be one of his friends.

– Paul Bowen

Since the dawn of time . . .
man has been fascinated by flight.
That fascination . . .
is a physical reflection . . .
of what we all long to return to.
We all fly in our dreams . . .
and when we awake . . .
we long for that inner freedom.
I hope the fantasy of flight . . .
helps light that spark within . . .
to continue you on our journey!

Kermit Weeks

The above saying has been on the entrance wall of *Fantasy of Flight* since the day we opened in 1995.

I learned a long time ago that not everybody likes airplanes, but everyone has a fascination for flight. Flight, more than anything, is the most profound metaphor of something we all relate to – *pushing our boundaries, reaching beyond ourselves,* and *freedom.*

This applies not only to the physical worlds that surround us, for we ALL relate to *reaching for the sky* and *reaching for the stars*; but it also applies to the worlds within us, for we also ALL relate to *soaring in our imagination* and *flying in our dreams.* Flight more than anything resonates to the core of our being and who we truly are!

This realization came to me over time as I pursued two parallel paths of interest that started early in life. One was a fascination with aircraft, history, and the physical aspects of outer flight; the other was a fascination with the worlds that surround us that we cannot see, and the inner aspects of flight.

I began building my first flyable airplane at age 17. Learning to fly at the same time, I also competed on my

High School Gymnastic Team. Since I was flipping around in the gym, it seemed only natural to begin flipping around in the sky. I began competing in a Bellanca Citabria and then a Decathlon with a dream of one day making the U.S. Aerobatic Team.

Aerobatics is the most profound expression of the metaphor of flight within the physical world. I not only pushed my boundaries and reached beyond myself with the airplanes I designed and built, but I pushed myself as a competitor within myself as well. From these experiences, I discovered a profound expression of freedom.

At the same time I began to explore the worlds within myself. In my mid-twenties I began to have out-of-body experiences. I floated through walls and ceilings and had limited success experiencing a world beyond this normal five-sense one. Some of what I had read about, I had now experienced. What I had read about and not experienced only made me want to pursue this path even more! From these experiences, I also discovered a profound freedom.

Aviators of past and present have always tapped into their sixth senses and other realities. This can come in the form of something as simple as a hunch, a sensation or a feeling that something is "not quite right." It might be a sense of knowing, but sometimes it can be much more. Charles Lindbergh, during his trans-Atlantic crossing, reported an experience of

Paul, Kermit and Dale "Snort" Snodgrass pose before flying a late day photo shoot during the annual gathering at Oshkosh, 2001.

In 2004, Kermit brought his P-40 seat to be signed by members of the AVG, Flying Tigers, who were meeting in Florida. *"May the Spirit of the AVG, 'Flying Tigers' be with whomever flies in this seat!"* was signed by L to R: Dick Rossi, Charlie Bond, Tex Hill, Bob Layher and Peter Wright.

being visited by *spirit entities* who guided and encouraged him as he desperately fought to stay awake and keep his plane on course. My life has become a fairy-tale and I now find myself living a similar Journey.

There is so much more to life than most people realize or are aware of. Our fascination with physical flight is a longing for that which we all do but don't necessarily realize it. We are actually multi-dimensional beings and all travel within other realities while we sleep. Most of us sense there is something to this but just can't quite pin it down. Each one of us is the

creator of our own reality, and within each one of us is an unbelievable amount of untapped potential.

Something draws each of us beyond ourselves and flight is its most profound metaphor. Humanity has *always* experienced this – a *hundred thousand years ago, today,* and in a *million years.* Everyone is drawn beyond themselves to be more tomorrow than they are today. I call this *fantasy of flight* and define it as, *that which draws us beyond what we think we are, to be more of what we truly are.* With *Fantasy of Flight* I hope to create a concept, a product, and a destination where people can self-discover their own potential!

I've met a kindred spirit with my good friend, Paul Bowen. We've done photo sessions together and he always comes up with awesome shots! His photos are like life itself, and you as well, if you look deep enough, will find much, much more. Paul's photos bring out that *fantasy of flight* within and evoke something inside, something that you might not be able to put your finger on.

Paul has put a lot of passion, heart, and soul into the following pages. His pictures will touch you in a way that other photographers find hard to replicate. As you turn the pages, open yourself to what sensations and feelings they might evoke. You will certainly be drawn to their beauty. You may find yourself longing for the freedom they express. You may even be touched in a way that might remind you of something lying deep within, that you have long forgotten!

Enjoy these great photographs, continue to fly in your dreams and, *I hope the fantasy of flight helps light that spark within to continue you on your Journey!*

– Kermit Weeks

INTRODUCTION

This book features the beauty of these Flying Sculptures and honors the owners and pilots who have invested their time, energy, passion and finances to keep these treasures flying. Unfortunately it does not begin to tell the full story of the sacrifice and commitment the men and women in the military and the civilian community endured during World War II or their contribution to the Freedoms we enjoy today.

I have spent the last 35 years as a commercial photographer specializing in advertising photography for the corporate aircraft manufacturers. I tell my four children, "Whatever you end up doing for a profession, do it with PASSION." I am incredibly fortunate to get paid for doing "my passion." When I started shooting airplanes in the early '70s, I had no idea what an adventurous life lay ahead. Most of us in the aviation community can honestly say it has brought us great adventures, deep friendships and wonderful stories to tell. I hope to share some of these with you in Volume IV, *Air to Air Mustangs and Corsairs.*

My first exposure to warbirds came through Tallmantz Aviation, based at Orange County Airport, California. Frank Pine and brother Walter became my regular pilots on photo flights while engineer Wayne Burtt kept us flying. My first B-25 mission was with Frank in one of the two Tallmantz Aviation B-25s. What an experience to step into that airplane and step back into history. Frank died in 1984, but I keep in close contact with Walt and his wife Marilyn. Frank's widow Martha, and her sister Ruth "Boots" Tallman – Frank Tallman's widow, sold the B-25s and most of the Tallmantz collection which was purchased by Kermit Weeks.

Over the years I've had the opportunity to shoot from 17 different B-25s. After Tallmantz Aviation sold their planes, I shot with Walt and the gang at The Air Museum Planes of Fame in Chino, California. Steve Hinton, John Maloney, John Hinton and Kevin Eldridge flew *Photo Fanny,* which for a while was aka *Betty Grable.* We've had a great time and

Paul's favorite spot to shoot from in the B-25 is the open air tail-gunner's position. It gets very cold, windy and noisy. When shooting, he must wear a headset for ear protection and communication with the pilots as he directs the target airplane. And yes, he is tethered in.

logged many hours watching beautiful sunsets and sunrises throughout the country. Steve Hinton, president of The Air Museum Planes of Fame, has flown nearly every plane in the collection and personally owns a P-51D Mustang. He won the Reno Air Races, flies frequently for television and feature films, and has been the target and platform pilot for numerous commercial and warbird shoots for me. Steve and his family have become my good friends.

After Frank Pine of Tallmantz Aviation died, and their B-25s were sold, Paul started working with brother Walter Pine and the pilots at The Air Museum Planes of Fame, in Chino, CA. Since then, they have become great friends. Pictured here with *Photo Fanny* and her modified nose job, are B-25 pilots John Maloney and young Steve Hinton, engineer Kyle Rohman, Citation pilots; Dan Grace, Wade Williams, Brendan Hartrett, Chad Johnson, Gary Read, Dave Shonka and Shannon Peterson; CJ3 owner Mike Herman and guest Frank Varasano; CJ1+ owner Arie DeJong and guests Jason DeJong, Leon DeNerii, Chuck Miller and Casey Miller; CJ2+ pilots Tim Maison and Nic Cherches; and Production Crew; Editor of *Directions Magazine* Ed Parrish, Sullivan Higdon & Sink Advertising Agency Art Director Jeff Filby, SHS videographer Derek Lowrey, still photographer Tom Jenkins and Paul.

Pilots Frank and Walter Pine with one of two B-25s owned by Tallmantz Aviation. This was the first of 17 B-25s Paul has shot from since 1975. Note the wrap-around glass nose which allowed a movie cameraman to pan a camera when the target plane was in the formation lead.

Under the guidance of close friend and B-25 instructor John Hinton, Paul gets to play in the left seat of *Photo Fanny* as Tom Jenkins observes.

My next exposure to warbirds came through Lee Lauderback who has become one of my closest friends. I met him while he was Arnold Palmer's chief pilot. After leaving Palmer, he started Stallion 51 Corp. with Doug Schultz, who has since passed away. Stallion 51, based in Kissimmee, Florida, started its Mustang orientation flights and training program centered around one of the few dual control TF-51 Mustangs, *Crazy Horse.* He has since added *Crazy Horse*[2] to the corral. Lee also hosted The Gathering of Mustangs and Legends in 1999, and The Gathering of Mustangs and Legends – The Final Round Up, in September, 2007, in Columbus, Ohio.

Warbird Digest's B-25 was used as the platform for many of the images in this book. B-25 owner and Magazine Publisher Tim Savage flew *The Green Dragon* with pilot Duane Carroll. Note the "stock" nose on the plane.

Paul's brother Lance created this illustration. Lance lives on Maui and is a graphic designer and cartoonist by trade. He also pastors Nu 'Oli Community Church in Lahaina.

Through Lee I met Kermit Weeks. Everyone in aviation knows of Kermit Weeks. Over the years he has amassed a great collection of airplanes. His aviation attraction, *Fantasy of Flight* in Polk City, Florida, is breathtaking. As I got to know Kermit, I became aware of some of his other talents and accomplishments. He is two-time U.S. National Aerobatics Champion, winner of silver medals in World Aerobatics competition, has designed and built airplanes – including one he started building at 17 and flew four years later.

Because the warbird community is so close knit, it wasn't long before I became friends with Dale "Snort" Snodgrass who is also based in Florida. Dale is a retired Navy commander who has amassed more time in F-14s than any other pilot in history. I've shot him (with my Canon) while he's flown his T-6, his F-86, and various Corsairs including Jim Read's and The Collings Foundation's. He has also been the platform pilot for me on warbird and commercial shoots. His professionalism and discipline in the cockpit make the shoot always go smoothly. You can see him regularly performing at airshows.

Tom Patten's Mustang works well as a mirror. Like Tom, the other owners of these award-winning airplanes not only put time, energy, and resources into the initial restoration, but also into their continuing upkeep.

Cessna Citation's *Directions Magazine* features owners and operators of Citations. Paul travels the world with *Directions* Editor Ed Parrish and Paul's long-time assistant/2nd photographer Tom Jenkins. They meet fascinating people who also have a love for aviation and an appreciation for corporate jets as business tools. Sydney Pollack is not only a film director, producer and actor, but he qualifies as a professional pilot, with over 3,000 hours of flight time. He flies left seat in his Citation X, often with copilot Ed Connelly.

Jack Roush has become one of my more recent friends. Famed NASCAR team owner, Jack also owns and flies two P-51 Mustangs. I first met him looking through my lens. As we flew together, and spent time together on the ground, I came to appreciate his passion for everything – that is, everything that has to do with quality. Whether it's quality of product, performance, or quality of life, Jack's there 200%. He appreciates and understands his privilege and responsibility in restoring and maintaining his airplanes. Gail and I and two of our children were guests of Jack's at a NASCAR race where one of his teams, with Mark Martin driving, won the race. We appreciated his hospitality in arranging for the victory. He is the ultimate host.

Bob Odegaard has the distinction of owning the only flying F2G Super Corsair. Only 10 were built at the end of WW II, and Bob's is the only one flying today. I met Bob at the Sun 'n Fun Airshow in Lakeland, Florida, in 2005. Bob was flying his Douglas C-47, painted bright yellow as *Duggy*, which has toured the U.S. in an attempt to interest young people in aviation. Later that year I visited Bob in North Dakota and shot him in his Mustang and Corsair. We had a great session. It's so much fun to fly with a professional and someone who is so enthusiastic about his passion for flying. You can't find a nicer guy.

After reading about Steve, Lee, Kermit, Dale, Jack and Bob, I'm sure you can see why I asked these friends to write their forewords for this book. I'm honored to call them friends, and truly appreciate what they've contributed to the aviation community and to the non-aviation community in gaining an understanding and appreciation for the role these warbirds have played in securing our Freedoms.

Saad Wallan, of Wallan Aviation in Riyadh, has become like a brother to Paul. A pilot, and owner of the largest car dealerships in Saudi Arabia, he also imports Cessnas into that region of the world. An accomplished pilot, Paul met Saad in 1996 when *Directions Magazine* featured him in an article. Saad's loving spirit is exemplified by the Christmas Day phone call Paul received from Riyadh, wishing Paul the best on that Holy Day.

Geriatric surfing in Maui – astronaut, air show performer, and surfer Robert "Hoot" Gibson, Chief Pilot Korbel Bros. and long-time friend of Paul's Gary Krambs, Paul's brother Lance Bowen, and Paul regroup after a summer surf session at Hot Sands, Puamana, Maui.

Once a surfer, always a surfer!

Bella is the first of the Bowen (Cook) grandchildren. Josh and Ashley can't decide if she should attend KSU or KU.

The Bowen Bunch 2004: Josh (Kansas State University) and Ashley (University of Kansas) Cook, Evan Senn (Wichita State University), Aubree (University of Kansas), Dylan Senn (Kansas State University), Gail (Ozark Bible College), Paul (University of California at Santa Barbara) and Chloé (Obedience School Dropout). I don't say lightly that God has blessed our lives. Those of you who know our children realize how fortunate Gail and I are. They're not perfect, but neither are their parents. I believe the success of our blended family is due to Gail and her unselfish attitude and our faith. She continues to be *the love of my life.*

I've made a lot of great friendships through aviation. I've worked with outstanding art directors, writers, and editors, as well as most of the airframe manufacturers and their advertising agencies creating countless brochures and ad campaigns for corporate aircraft. I am also credited with over 900 magazine covers. But whether shooting corporate jets or warbirds, producing these photos is a team effort. Hopefully, through the group photos and individual pilot portraits in the book, you can share in the experience of "the team."

There's a quality of people involved in aviation that is rarely found. The people I deal with daily have the kind of character traits I want my children to have. I know if I have a problem, I can call numerous aviation friends who will help immediately. It's wonderful to be a part of a community that cares.

My thanks go out to all the pilots and behind-the-scenes people who made this compilation of images possible.

As we remember those lost during World War II and after, may we appreciate their lives and sacrifices for us.

I hope my book brings you hours of visual enjoyment and years of thoughtful remembrances.

This picture conveys the spirit of this book – an appreciation of the time, energy and finances dedicated to the refurbishment and preservation of these *Flying Sculptures* called warbirds, and, a desire to respect and acknowledge all that The Greatest Generation has given to us to secure the Freedoms we enjoy today. Pictured here are Mustang owner and pilot Jack Roush, his daughter Susan Roush-McClenaghan and her husband Dale McClenaghan.

To my parents' generation
who gave so much
even their lives
to secure the Freedoms we enjoy today –
And to those of my generation
who keep the Flying Sculptures in the air
and help us remember the past –
Plus a special note of appreciation to our troops
who are currently serving in Harm's Way

C O N T E N T S

1

MUSTANGS
P-51A, P-51C & TF-51

MUSTANG FOREWORD
BY LEE LAUDERBACK

Stallion 51's Chief TF-51 Instructor and Demo Pilot Lee Lauderback, started flying in 1966, when he was 15. He is one of the pilots for the U.S. Air Force Heritage Flight Program and a civilian instructor for the Navy Test Pilot School at Patuxent River, Maryland, where test pilot students learn their craft flying the Mustang.

Shortly after Lee graduated from college, he started to work for noted professional golfer and businessman Arnold Palmer, heading up Arnie's flight operations as chief pilot and director of flight operations for 16 years. There, he flew Learjets, Cessna Citation business jets, and an MD500E helicopter.

It was a great start for a terrific career.

Over the past 40-plus years, Lee has amassed more than 18,000 flying hours, over 6,000 of them in Mustangs, which makes him the world's high-time Mustang pilot, plus he has acquired time in the F-15 Eagle, F-16 Viper, and F/A-18 Hornet. He is a certified flight and ground instructor for single and multi-engine aircraft, instrument, helicopters, and gliders; he is an FAA pilot proficiency examiner; and he performs acceptance test flights in various warbirds, helicopters, and turbojets.

Additionally, Lee has piloted sailplanes for more than 2,000 hours, competed in many soaring contests, and set several sailplane records.

He is also an accomplished falconer, having earned his federal and state falconry licenses. His interest lies in "maintaining, improving and ultimately releasing the bird back into the wild." Lee has recently built a home in Idaho, which will allow him to take his falconry interests into a new location.

When I think about Lee, I think *professional.* Everything he does is done well. I also think of *safety.* Lee has saved many lives with his Mustang training. And I think of *friendship.* Lee is one of my closest friends.

– Paul Bowen

With slide rules and engineering genius, North American Aviation built the P-51 Mustang in less than 120 days. Conceived as a weapon of war to defend democracy, the remarkable Mustang became arguably the premier fighter of World War II. Today the Mustang is approaching its 70th birthday, and we can only imagine the different pilots who flew them, places they went, and missions each of these Mustangs in these pages flew during the war years.

Only a few Mustangs returned to the United States after World War II, but new ones quickly went off to another war. Fresh Mustangs came off the assembly line for combat in Korea, primarily for air-to-ground missions, but occasionally they went up against Communist MiG-15s.

Then, after the Korean Armistice, the P-51 continued its military service in Air National Guard units across the United States and in air forces around the world. Finally in 1985, after almost 45 years of military service, the last Mustang retired from the Dominican air force, and its days as a combat aircraft were over. Of course, that didn't even come close to ending its flying career.

Civilian pilots had already been flying Mustangs for sport, racing, air shows, and other purposes since the late 1950s, high performance fighters sold to them as military surplus for a fraction of the government's original $56,000 price tag. But they were largely amateurs, and they flew like amateurs.

Unlike their military predecessors, most civilian Mustang pilots weren't properly trained. Consequently, Mustang accident statistics were unacceptably high, annually 10 percent of airworthy Mustangs; and in most cases, pilot error was the cause.

In those days Mustangs were inexpensive and easy to buy, just surplus military junk – and often treated just that casually. Careless owners took them out for an occasional spin and left them outside to deteriorate. It was a sign of the times in the United States' affluent, then-new "throw away" society; and the Mustang's future looked bleak.

But then a new breed of owner came to the rescue. Well-heeled individuals with deep respect for history saw the Mustang's real value.

They began buying those old, worn-out Mustangs and making the substantial investments necessary to restore them to pristine, like-new combat condition, maintain them properly, and operate them professionally. They replaced every nut and bolt. They polished the air-frames with tender loving care. They replaced civilian paint jobs with original combat-unit paint schemes and personalized each one to pay tribute to the most famous combat aces. This new breed of Mustang owners transformed their P-51s into national treasures so they could take their rightful place in history, so Mustangs with names like *Angels' Playmate*, *Old Crow*, *Glamorous Glen III*, *Hell-er Bust*, *American Beauty*, and *Slender, Tender & Tall* once again flew.

In April, 1999, Lee and Stallion 51 hosted the *Gathering of Mustangs and Legends* at their home base in Kissimmee, Florida, featuring 65 Mustangs and 12 Legends from World War II.

Sometimes at the owners' invitations, the aces who fought in those Mustangs took to air again in the very craft restored to honor them. Colonel Bruce Carr, Colonel Bud Anderson, and many others once again took the Mustangs' controls. This time though, they were far from war. This time it was purely for fun – to enjoy the freedoms they themselves had preserved.

The new breed of Mustang owners and pilots also took highly professional attitudes toward their initial and recurrent training. They invested the time and money necessary to learn how to fly their high performance machines, and they reduced high loss rate due to accidents. The stories of torque rolls on go-around and excessive rudder required for take-off faded as well-trained pilots began to understand and employ proper procedures, procedures they learned in TF-51s, the dual-cockpit, dual-controlled Mustangs such as *Crazy Horse.*

Soon, thanks to this new kind of owner and pilot, the number of flying Mustangs began to grow for the first time since initial production, and it continues to grow today.

In September, 2007, *Stallion 51 Corporation* in coopera-tion with the Columbus Regional Airport Authority host-ed *The Gathering of Mustangs and Legends - The Final Roundup*, at Rickenbacker International Airport in Columbus, Ohio. Many World War II combat veterans and their great grandchildren marveled at a lineup of over 100 extraordinary Mustangs and 51 Legends, including Aces, crew chiefs, WASPs and others who were part of the P-51 family.

Today the P-51 Mustang has a bright future, or so it

would seem; but we can't afford to be complacent. We have an enemy to defeat, and its name is *stupidity*. Well-meaning but shortsighted and misinformed Congressional legislators still threaten our Mustangs with unpatriotic "demilitarization" legislation. Such laws would require us to destroy surplus military articles now in civilian ownership – including our Mustangs – historic artifacts we have devoted our efforts and fortunes to preserve and protect. We must "keep our heads on a swivel," remain vigilant, and meet every single one of these threats in classic fighter pilot style – *head on.*

I am truly blessed to have flown the Mustang almost every day for the past 15 years, to have the opportuni-ty to give back some of the freedom and joy the Mustang has given me, to share the Mustang with so many others who would never have had the chance to experience the performance and handling qualities of this thoroughbred.

I remind myself often I am just *the keeper of the keys.*

These treasures must move on to the next generation, not because they are awe-some to fly, but because they represent what so many fallen patriots gave their lives to defend.

Our Mustangs represent the ultimate freedom.

– Lee Lauderback

P-51A Mustang

Anyone who knows about World War II understands the important role the Mustang played in successfully ending the war with victory for the Allies. The Mustang was the premier fighter of the War. It was used as a long-range bomber escort, a dog fighter, and a ground-attack airplane. The P-51A, B and C models had razorback cockpits, which were replaced in the D by a glass bubble canopy to give the pilot all-around visibility.

This airplane, owned by The Air Museum Planes of Fame in Chino, California, is one of only a few flying in the world. Shown here in three different paint schemes, pilots John Maloney and John Hinton fly tight formation on the photo planes.

Note the three-bladed prop on the Allison engine powered A model. It was replaced on the D model with a four-bladed prop attached to the Rolls-Royce Merlin engine. There's nothing like the sound of that engine and prop as the Mustang flies by. You don't have to look up to know it's a Mustang going by – but everybody does.

I am writing this with tears in my eyes. It's Saturday, July 28, 2007, and I came to the studio to work on this book. After checking my e-mail, I was shocked to learn that Gerald "Gerry" Beck, owner and pilot of this P-51A, died yesterday at Oshkosh. I'm not ashamed to say I broke down and cried.

There are a lot of wonderful people in aviation, but Gerry was near the top of the list. Somehow, he seemed to balance his love for airplanes and flying with a close family life. The sparkle in his eyes and his enthusiasm for everything were so contagious.

The first time I shot Gerry, he was flying his Corsair at a gathering in Indiana. Our second session was also in the Corsair at an event in Connecticut. Besides being a great formation pilot, Gerry was easy to work with – professional and anything *but* a prima donna. Tim Savage, publisher of *Warbird Digest* magazine, took me to Wahpeton, North Dakota, on two occasions to shoot Gerry and his best friend Bob Odegaard. Each owned and flew a Corsair and a Mustang. These images were shot in August, 2006. Gerry had just finished building the A model and I got to shoot it from Tim's Beech Baron with the doors removed.

I am so sorry for the loss to Gerry's wonderful wife, Cindy, and daughter Whitney. It was my honor to know a man so rare.

P-51C Mustang

The P-51B and C models were powered by Rolls-Royce Merlin engines, which allowed them to perform at high altitudes, for long distances, and at high speeds. This improved Mustang changed the war in Europe. Now the Mustang could escort the bombers all the way from England to Germany and back.

Kermit Weeks' *Ina the Macon Belle*, painted in the only Tuskegee Ace Lt. Col. Lee Archer's paint scheme, was awarded Warbirds Grand Champion at Oshkosh during the Experimental Aircraft Association's AirVenture 2001. EAA's annual gathering is the highlight of the air show season for many pilots and enthusiasts.

Doug Rozendaal flew off Kermit's wing in the Commemorative Air Force's *Tuskegee Airmen* C model. This was a rare flight, because at the time of this shoot, these were the only two P-51C Mustangs flying in the world.

The CAF *Tuskegee Airmen* P-51C, also known as *The Red Tail Project*, participated as an outreach program to youth throughout the country by flying and exhibiting the airplane to get their attention, then sharing the message of "going after your dreams." Many dedicated volunteers had put time into restoring the plane, keeping it flying, and showing it whenever possible.

I had the privilege of flying with pilot Don Hinz during the Centennial Celebration at Kitty Hawk on December 16, 2003. My old friend Doug Rozendaal, who also flew *The Red Tail*, arranged for me to fly over the memorial during the celebration festivities. Loaded with my Canon in Jim Tobul's SNJ, we departed a nearby airport and made several passes by the memorial with the SNJ canopy open. Don flew perfect formation as Tobul relayed my positioning requests. I immediately knew I was working with a pro. We finished our passes, joined up with another plane for a few images, and then flew back to base. Job completed, we headed off to a party to celebrate.

On May 29, 2004, while performing at an air show, *The Red Tail* suffered an engine failure, and Don Hinz lost his life in the resulting crash. Don was a dedicated professional, a true gentleman and a devoted family man. His widow, Pat, and their four sons and large family, can be proud of Don's life and that his final courageous act was to guide his crippled airplane away from the crowd.

Since that sad day in May, 2004, great progress has been made in restoring the Mustang by CAF volunteers and by Gerry Beck at his Tri-State Aviation facility. Nothing can replace the loss of life; and now with Gerry gone, too, it's difficult to think about restorations.

However, John Beyl, crew chief for the Mustang, said it beautifully in an article appearing in the Fall 2005 issue of *Warbird Digest*. He wrote: "As I write this article, it's mid-May and only days before the one year anniversary of the tragic loss of Don Hinz and the Commemorative Air Force's C-model Mustang. After several false starts, in frustration I pushed the keyboard away, took a few minutes to think about *The Red Tail Project* and reflect on the incredible progress that's been made in the last year. It quickly occurred to me that in the same fighting spirit of the Tuskegee Airmen, rebuilding this rare Mustang is all about overcoming overwhelming odds to send a message of courage and hope. If there ever was a Phoenix to rise from the ashes, *The Red Tailed Mustang* and her crew would certainly qualify."

Donations for the restoration and upcoming operating costs of *The Red Tail* are appreciated and needed: www.redtail.org

Max Chapman, Jr., currently owns three Mustangs. His most recent restoration is this P-51C. It could be classified as a TP-51C, the T standing for Trainer, because of the second instrument panel and controls installed at Max's request. Most of the outstanding restorations being completed these days are a compilation of parts from numerous old airplanes, plus newly created parts. It's time consuming and expensive. The craftsmen working on these flying sculptures are, in fact, *sculptors*. Restoration has been elevated to a fine art form. And it's businessmen and aviators like Max who dedicate their time, energy and resources to further their love, passion and commitment to saving the history they represent.

I was at Oshkosh in 2005 when I first saw the C. Ed Shipley agreed to fly a photo sortie in the C while Lee Lauderback flew Max's D. I know Ed and Lee well, so I knew I was in for a great session. Both are great guys and outstanding formation pilots with years of experience flying Mustangs and flying tight formation together. Max and I hopped into the *Warbird Digest magazine's* B-25 and headed for Lake Winnebago.

Well, the pictures tell it all. When you have the right subject, with the right pilots, in the right setting, you can't miss.

Before every flight we have an extensive briefing. I start by stating what I hope to achieve artistically, and then the pilots discuss how to achieve that safely. I tell them where I want to go, what altitude, what time for wheels-in-the-well, if there's more than one plane, what order they'll form together, and so on. The pilots then fine-tune and respond to my requests, and we head off for a safe and successful mission.

This was an historic flight because Max had all three of his Mustangs available and they represented three models: P-51C with Ed Shipley, P-51D with Eric Huppert and TF-51 (Trainer-Fighter) with Lee Lauderback.

Partway through the mission, the B-25 intercom became inoperable so no one could hear my directions as to where to place the target Mustangs. By using hand signals I directed them as best I could. These guys flew outstanding formation, as they were trained to do, and finished the session as we created art. Truly, the pilots are the heroes of any photo shoot.

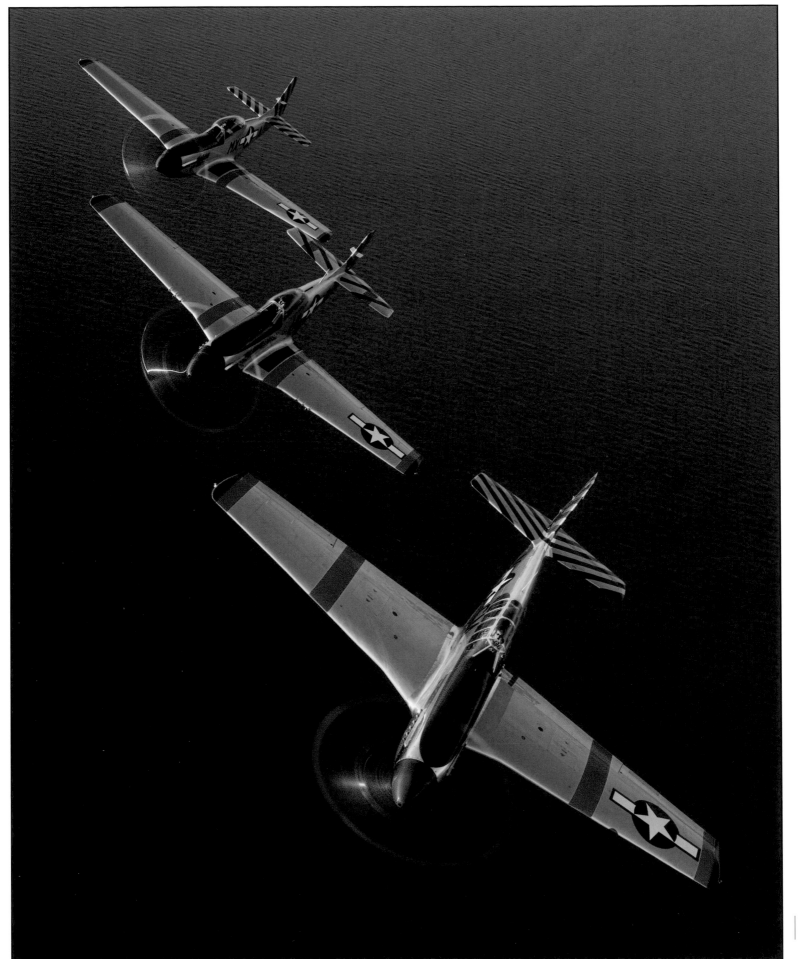

TF-51 MUSTANG

In 1994, *Crazy Horse* was the first warbird I ever shot air-to-air. The TF, or Trainer-Fighter version of the Mustang, is fitted with a second seat, complete instrument panel, and dual-controls. At its base in Kissimmee, Florida, Stallion 51 operates *Crazy Horse* and *Crazy Horse2*, specializing in orientation flights, checkout training, unusual attitude training, military contracts, air shows and aircraft management.

I first met Lee Lauderback in 1987 when he was Arnold Palmer's chief pilot. I was shooting a story on Palmer at the time. Because Lee flew helicopters, sailplanes, corporate jets and warbirds, I recommended him to *Flying Magazine* to be the subject of a "Flying Reader" house ad featuring interesting pilots who read the magazine. Our friendship evolved and today, he and Angela West are two of Gail's and my closest friends.

Lee's obsession with flying safely suits his job perfectly. When someone comes to Lee for training or simply an orientation session, you know you will be safe and get the best experience possible. Lee holds the distinction of having logged more Mustang hours than anyone – ever – with over 6,000 hours.

Crazy Horse² joined Stallion 51 in 2005. It had previously been owned by Dick Thurman and known as *Kentucky Babe*. Another TF-51, it is also being used for training and air shows. There are currently an estimated 16 dual-control Mustangs flying throughout the world.

With a love for aviation, specifically the Mustang and the people who built them, maintained them, and flew them, Lee organized the Gathering of Mustangs and Legends in 1999. The event was held at the Stallion 51 facility at Kissimmee, where it drew 65 Mustangs and honored 12 Legends who had flown them.

In September, 2007, The Gathering of Mustangs and Legends – The Final Roundup, drew an even larger crowd at Columbus, Ohio. The sacrifice these heroes made for our country should never be forgotten.

Almost all of the current TF-51 Mustangs were restoration/conversions from D models. *Kentucky Babe* was one such award-winning example. When Dick Thurman purchased the plane, it had been a Reno Air Racer and needed a lot of repairs to undo the racing modifications. Wanting his pilot friends to fly it also, he converted it to a TF. The end result was a spectacular restoration.

These shots are good examples of two styles of shooting. The "power shot" below was taken with a telephoto lens to compress the image while the photo platform and subject plane orbited in left-hand 360° turns. The other image was taken with a wide-angle lens as Lee Lauderback flew in close to the tail of the B-25 platform. I don't let just anybody get that close to me in flight.

Mad Max, the TF-51 owned and flown by Max Chapman, Jr., divides its time between Jackson, Wyoming, and Kissimmee, Florida, when it's not at air shows. Max's first award-winning warbird was his incredible Corsair, followed by *Mad Max*. To catch this formation as they flew past the Grand Tetons, I shot from the wedged-open door of a vintage Beech Staggerwing biplane. Max, Lee Lauderback, and John Muszala claim honors for this image.

Because of the close friendship of Max and Lee, they fly together often. The picture on the right was shot at the 1999 Gathering of Mustangs. A shot from this series appeared on the cover of *Air and Space Smithsonian Magazine*.

2

P51-D Mustangs

P-51D FOREWORD
BY STEVE HINTON

The Air Museum Planes of Fame President Steve Hinton was one of the original "Chino kids," a member of that band of warbird-smitten young boys who earned their flight time working at museum back when it was in Claremont, California, and following it to Buena Park and then, in 1965, to its now-permanent home at Chino Airport.

In addition to rebuilding warbirds, Steve's restoration company, Fighter Rebuilders, consults on restorations and preservation of these rare machines as well as operations including motion pictures and airshows.

Steve is a member in good standing of the Screen Actors Guild and is highly respected in Hollywood. He has flown for countless feature motion pictures, movies made for television, television series, and commercials. His film credits include the long-running television series, *Baa Baa Blacksheep*, and such box office hits as *The Rocketeer*, and *Pearl Harbor*.

Steve is equally famous and respected in professional aviation circles for his photographic memory of anything having to do with airplanes, superb judgment and airmanship, spot-on precision flying, and for keeping his absolute cool even under the most desperate conditions – like the day *Red Baron RB-51* took second place at Reno, and then lost power. That day, Steve's final radio call of the flight was a calm, "Race control, I have a problem;" and then he flew the airplane as far into the crash as he could. Though he saved his life, he put himself into the hospital with a broken back, leg, and ankle among other injuries.

Subsequently flying John Sandberg's purpose-built *Tsunami* and All Coast Racing Team's *Super Corsair*, Steve competed as an Unlimited race pilot for a total of 13 years, winning the Gold National Championships in 1978 in the *Red Baron RB-51* and in 1985 in the *Super Corsair*. In 1978, Steve was 26, and he's still the youngest competitor ever to win the Gold Race. Additionally, in 1979 flying *Red Baron RB-51*, Steve set the World Speed Record for piston powered aircraft of 499.046 miles per hour – a record which stood for 10 years; and in that same aircraft, he became the only pilot in history ever to win four Unlimited races within a one-year period.

He's also a great guy and a lot of fun to work with, and the perfect authority to open this next chapter.

– Paul Bowen

People fly for one reason – to go *fast*.

So naturally, aviation has a rich history of races. Many of the early ones were devoted to serious cross-continent and continent-to-continent challenges and later, after the pioneering achievement of making the distance, to speed runs.

But today, air racing is more like stock car racing was in its beginning. Our best race pilots are highly skilled technical flyers, experts at wringing top performance out of specially restored and tricked-out World War II fighters traversing tight, pylon-marked courses. It's a sport you win by thousandths of a second. And no matter how good a pilot you are, your airplane had better be the fastest thing in the sky that day, or you're going to lose.

Which is why there would be *no* air races without the P-51 Mustang.

Though the Mustang flew with the Air Force for many years after World War II and had an even longer international military career, many came onto the surplus market just after World War II – often for prices around $1,500. Former wartime pilots and private pilots bought many of them, and so did the first post-war air racers.

The Mustang is a speed demon. It looks like one. It sounds like one. And it's been winning air races since 1947.

Film stunt pilot Paul Mantz created the most prominent of the early Mustang racers when he turned his surplus P-51C model into *Blaze of Noon*. He sealed the wings so he could fill them with fuel, which extended his range and eliminated drag-inducing drop tanks. Mantz flew *Blaze of Noon* to victory in the 1946 and 1947 Bendix Air Races and in 1947 set a new U.S. coast-to-coast speed record.

Later, when Mantz sold *Blaze of Noon* to Charles Blair, who would later marry movie star Maureen O'Hara, Blair renamed it *Excalibur III*.

In 1951, flying *Excalibur III*, Blair first set a New York-to-London record; and then, in a paradigm-shifting achievement, he won the Harmon Trophy when he flew from Norway to Fairbanks, Alaska. That flight proved Blair's contention it was possible to make such a flight over the magnetic pole by using sun sights for navigation – and it made the Air Force change its mind about guarding against a Soviet air strike from the north, something previously considered impossible.

Steve has the distinction of currently being the only insured person authorized to fly owner Rod Lewis' unique P-38, *Glacier Girl*.

That particular Mustang is now on display at the National Air and Space Museum's Steven F. Udvar-Hazy Center.

It's the granddaddy of all Mustang racers, and it started the pot boiling for the rest of us in this game.

I myself began racing a quarter of a century later in 1976 flying a P-63 King Cobra, then in 1977, I got to fly my first real racer, Ed Browning's Rolls-Royce Griffin powered *Red Baron RB-51* with contra-rotating props. *Red Baron RB-51* was a fantastic airplane – very fast – and in it, I had some significant successes.

Then at Reno in 1979, I nearly killed myself in it.

But, boy was I ever hooked on the races – and on warbirds.

Of course, one of the most enjoyable parts of racing competition has been rebuilding warbirds, both as precision restorations and hotrods. And I'm proud to say our Fighter Rebuilders Hangar has restored more than 40 of the World War II aircraft currently flying.

I don't race warbirds anymore, but I still take part in the Reno Air Races every year flying the T-33 jet pace plane, and I keep busy both restoring warbirds and flying them for motion picture productions.

As you can probably tell, I love airplanes.

I also love flying for my buddy, Paul Bowen's camera. Paul knows more about how to make these great machines look fantastic than anybody, and he always runs a professional, safe photo shoot.

What a pleasure to fly for him.

And what an honor to provide this narrative.

I hope you enjoy the sights you're about to see in this chapter.

– Steve Hinton

In 2005, The *Discovery Wings* Channel presented a program rating the Top Ten Fighters ever built. With competition like the F-16 Eagle and F-22 Raptor, the Mustang placed first! The P-51D was the last model of Mustang built. Fitted with the Rolls-Royce Merlin engine and six machine guns, it was fast, maneuverable, and deadly.

It also had the range to escort bombers from England to Germany and back. The Mustang was first requested in 1940 by England for that very purpose. These Merlin equipped fighters performed at high altitude much better than the first A models, providing escort to B-17s and B-24s on their bombing raids deep into enemy territory. By the end of the War, Mustangs destroyed nearly 5,000 enemy aircraft.

It was fitting that in 2003, Mustang owner, pilot, and former Jaguar race driver Bob Tullius donated his Mustang to the Royal Air Force Museum. *Donald Duck* was painted to represent and honor Captain Donald R. Emerson who was killed in action on Christmas Day in 1944. Tullius is quoted as saying, "it seems only appropriate that Donald should be remembered in the country from which he flew in those difficult days. He and many others like him should never be forgotten."

The Cavanaugh Flight Museum's Mustang, shown at the right, was flown by Aubrey Hair behind the B-25. I don't think there's a bad angle to photograph on this plane. Sometimes I have to try very hard to make a plane look sleek and fast, but not the Mustang.

Rod Lewis understands quality of life. Achieving success in his oil business based in southern Texas, Rod worked hard and gambled with high stakes, and he won, which enables him to be financially secure. Now he can spend more time with his wonderful family and friends, and he can enjoy his long-running passion – flying!

In addition to his two Citations, which are business tools, Rod has amassed a large collection of pristine warbirds, which continues to grow. At his Jardin Ranch, located between Laredo and San Antonio, Texas, he has built a 27,000 square foot hangar adjacent to the 5,400 foot-long, 80 foot-wide private airstrip. Each year he invites his buddies for fun, flying, and food – Texas Style. Even in those years he was battling Stage III cancer, Lewis insisted the fly-in must go on!

What could be more fun than flying with friends? Rod and John Penney, of Reno Air Racing fame, flew in *La Pistolera*, with close friend Mark Huffstutler in his Mustang, followed by Todd Steward and Fred Cabanas in *Luscious Lisa*. Rod's most recent addition to his "air force" was revealed at the 2007 fly-in, when Steve Hinton arrived in the most famous of all P-38s, *Glacier Girl*.

Ike Enns formed up on *Old Glory*, the B-25 then owned by Russ Newman and also based in Tulsa, Oklahoma. *Miracle Maker* hung tight as I circled to get the last light of the day. This was shot from the open canopy of a North American AT-6G, owned and flown by Alden Miller.

Spam Can and *Wee Willy II* are stable mates. *Spam Can* was one of the early acquisitions at The Air Museum Planes of Fame in Chino, California. Ed Maloney, who founded the museum in January, 1957, bought this P-51D in November of that same year. All three of his children have been deeply involved in the museum. They were part of "the Chino kids" who have had a great influence on the warbird community over the past decades. Son Jim was killed on May 21, 1983, flying a Ryan PT-22. He and best friend Steve Hinton had started Fighter Rebuilders, a restoration shop based at the museum. Younger son John Maloney flies everything the museum owns, and is vice president of POF. Daughter Karen is the director of development, and married Steve Hinton, who is currently president of the museum. This family endeavor continues with Steve's brother John, working with Fighter Rebuilders and also flying most of the museum's planes and Steve's son, Steve, also flying the warbirds.

Wee Willy II is owned by Steve Hinton, and in the photo across the page, brother John is flying, with my wife, Gail, seated in the back. So you can see, the warbird community is very family oriented. I should mention that Steve Hinton, John Maloney, John Hinton, and Kevin Eldridge have flown me numerous times in the POF B-25 *Photo Fanny*. They're great pilots, hard workers and great pals of mine.

Alan Anderson owned and flew *Su Su* when I shot him flying low over the marshlands near Jacksonville, Florida. It was a challenge to find a background that complemented the paint scheme. When former Apollo astronaut Frank Borman owned the airplane, he had *Su Su* painted in these Korean War-era markings of the 44th FS, Clark AFB, in the Philippines.

The pilots of the target planes need to be formation-qualified to make the shoot run safely and productively. It also helps a lot if the photo platform plane that I'm shooting from has formation pilots. My pilots in the Beech Baron twin-piston platform were Patty Wagstaff and Dale "Snort" Snodgrass. Patty is three-time U.S. National Aerobatic Champion, and currently a regular airshow performer. Dale was a Navy commander, is the high-time F-14 pilot, and is also a prolific airshow performer.

Bob Baker grew up in Oklahoma and after college, he farmed with his grandfather. During high school and college he had worked for a company that rebuilt helicopters. That's where he got his knowledge of aircraft. By age 23, he was designing and manufacturing farm machinery. To increase business, he learned to fly and bought several general aviation single and twin pistons. Then he went to Oshkosh.

The Experimental Aircraft Association holds its annual AirVenture fly-in at Oshkosh, Wisconsin. When Bob joined a friend at OSH in 1993, he couldn't even identify a Mustang. A short time later, he owned a Mustang "project" which he completed restoring in 2000, and sold in 2005. In the mean time, he'd started restoring a second Mustang. After devoting seven to eight thousand hours of his own time to the airplane over a four year period, he completed it in 2003.

Deciding to honor Major General Cuthbert A. "Bill" Pattillo, who flew 35 combat missions in Mustangs, Baker named the plane *Sweet and Lovely*. Pattillo was shot down on April 10, 1945, and spent the remainder of the War as a POW. Bill and his twin brother, Lt. Gen. Charles C. "Buck" Pattillo, were instrumental in forming the USAF demonstration team, the Thunderbirds.

In 2004, *Sweet and Lovely* won The Grand Champion Warbird, World War II category, at Oshkosh. Bob also earned a Golden Wrench trophy for the restoration. Today, he tours airshows and has become active with the Kansas Aviation Museum in Wichita, Kansas.

Dick James was an excellent pilot and a fine man. Sadly, we lost Dick in July, 2005, when he was killed in a Mustang crash.

Donna-Mite had two paint schemes. The picture to the right was the older one. Normally, the target pilot should never lose sight of the lead plane. But, during our preflight briefing, we agreed that Dick would stage-back farther than normal and start high at our 7:00 position and move to our 5:00 as I shot with a longer lens. By tilting the camera, I added more motion to the image.

I had flown with Dick on several occasions and considered him a friend. The day before his tragedy, he invited me to come stay at his home in a few months and shoot a gathering of planes that would be meeting for a fly-in.

Chuck Greenhill has been involved in the war-bird community for many years. He owns and flies numerous warbirds, including two P-51Ds – *Geraldine* and *Lou IV*. Chuck flew formation at Oshkosh with Dick James in *Donna-Mite* and Jack Roush in *Old Crow*.

Nathan Davis' highly polished *Checkertail Clan* is based in Kokomo, Indiana. Doug Fisher flew *Checkertail Clan* as the CAF Mustang pulled underneath. The alternating black and white stripes on the wings were painted on the allied airplanes to help quickly identify them as friendlies during the invasion of Normandy on D-Day, June 6, 1944.

Nathan flew it single-ship in 2005 over Lake Winnebago. Many of the owners of these great airplanes are generous enough to take passengers along for their *dream flight*.

I first met Bob Jepson in 1986, while on assignment for Cessna Citation's *Directions Magazine*. The magazine features owners and operators of Citations, and Bob has owned a few. Currently he flies a Citation X, the world's fastest business jet. But Bob loves his Mustangs, too.

He has owned four Mustangs at one time, more than anyone else except the U.S. Government – *Lady Alice, Diamond Back, Little Witch* and *Hell-er Bust*. I shot Lee Lauderback flying *Hell-er Bust*, which is painted in authentic markings to honor triple ace Capt. Edwin Heller.

It's actually quite difficult to photograph a highly polished airplane in flight. The metal acts like a mirror and will reflect everything. The "hot-spots" from the sun can make or break the shot. I try to catch a glint of light to show the polished surface, but I'm careful not to overdo it or the film or pixels can't record the bright contrast.

All of Bob's Mustangs have been award winners, including his most recent restoration *Little Witch*, which garnished top honors as Post World War II Grand Champion at the EAA Sun 'n Fun event held in Lakeland, Florida, during April, 2003. Bob stated: "Preserving these national treasures is great fun, a true labor of love and most gratifying. The day will come that it passes into the hands of a new owner. Hopefully, that person will feel, along with the joy of ownership, the responsibility of the care and upkeep that comes with these magnificent warbirds."

Tom Wood, owner of a chain of car dealerships in the Indianapolis area, has a fine collection of warbirds, including an F-86F Sabre, an F-8F Bearcat and this P-51D Mustang. Having served in the Royal Canadian Air Force, the Mustang was purchased by Woods in 1969 and continues to be flown by him. Tom is a warbird owner who not only puts his time and money into restorations, but makes time to keep current in flying them, and sharing them at airshows.

The Commemorative Air Force, or CAF, is dedicated to keeping warbirds flying. One of its P-51s, *Gunfighter,* flies a busy air show schedule each year. Its primary pilot, Brig. Gen. Reg Urschler, logged over 13,000 flying hours during his 32 years of service in the United States Air Force. Reg is easily identified as the Mustang pilot who displays a large American flag as he taxies his plane. For this aerial shoot, Captain Larry Lumpkin piloted *Gunfighter.*

The CAF has estimated the hourly operating costs of the Mustang to approach "$1,600, which includes the cost of engine overhaul, parts, maintenance, insurance, hangar, fuel, oil, paint and all the other items necessary to operate the aircraft safely." Donations are always appreciated.

The *City of Winnipeg* is currently the only Mustang with Canadian markings. When owner Bob May was a kid growing up on a farm in Manitoba, he got his first close-up view of an airplane. It was a P-51D Mustang. In fact, there were about 15 of them in storage after being discarded by the Royal Canadian Air Force.

May's career in aviation included owning Keewatin Air in the arctic, which started out flying deHavilland Beavers and Cessna 185s and, more recently, flew Pilatus PC-12s and King Air B200s. But through the years, he never lost his love for the Mustang. Then in 1990, he started buying Mustang parts and went to Uruguay in 1991 to salvage a wreck and begin a restoration project. Complications arose, but finally in 1994 he shipped the remains back to the United States.

It takes a lot of time, resources, and people to complete a restoration properly. Gerry Beck's Tri-State Aviation in Wahpeton, North Dakota, was the primary contractor, working initially on the fuselage. Bob Odegaard at Odegaard Aviation built the wings using castings and brackets from the wreckage. Once the fuselage was together, it was sent to Mike Vadeboncoeur at Midwest Aero Restorations in Danville, Illinois, for the detail work. The engine was discovered in storage in Quebec. A tailcone was found in a barn in Winnipeg. But it all came together at Gerry Beck's when, in August, 2004, the *City of Winnipeg* flew with Bob Odegaard at the controls.

The following four pages, 64-67, feature Bob Odegaard flying his Mustang, *Dazzling Donna*.

I've known Dr. Hank Reichert for more than 20 years. When I first met him, he owned a 1929 Great Lakes bi-plane, and a Beechcraft Duke. Since then, he has graduated to a Mustang. His close friend, Paul Ehlen, caught the bug through Hank, and now each of them has a P-51D. Hank's *Dakota Kid II*, and Paul's *Little Horse* were both built-up at Gerry Beck's Tri-State Aviation. In August, 2005, I had the chance to go to North Dakota to shoot them both on a special occasion.

Dakota Kid II was painted to honor its pilot, Noble Peterson. Peterson returned to South Dakota after the War and became a rancher. *Little Horse* was painted to honor its pilot, Ken Dahlberg, a triple ace, who was shot down three times. Dahlberg resides in Minneapolis, as does Paul Ehlen.

Reichert and Ehlen arranged to have Peterson and Dahlberg join them for flights in *their* airplanes. The *Warbird Digest* B-25 took the lead with four excited Mustang pilots in tow. After the flight, Dahlberg stated that the flight had been the highlight of his year.

On a personal note, I had met Ken Dahlberg at the 1999 Gathering of Mustangs and Legends. He was one of the honored legends. I liked him immediately. He is an accomplished businessman, having started Miracle Ear, and he continues to fly his CitationJet. But, his smile and the twinkle in his eye are what caught my attention.

It's always fun and a challenge to shoot more than one plane in formation. I keep saying that the true heroes of any air-to-air photo session are the pilots. This becomes even more true when you put more planes together. A photo shoot is no place to practice formation flying. The pilots must have the skills and experience and trust in each other to position their planes where I need them to be for the best possible photos.

There are normal positions that pilots fly off each other, but that might not look good to the camera. The pilots trust each other to do their jobs safely and expertly. They must also trust me – so when I request they move up or down five feet, or forward or back 10 feet, I am going to get *the* shot that we will all be proud of.

I salute these pilots for a great shoot: Al Schiffer flying Ken Wagnon's *Cripes A' Mighty*, Tom Patten flying his *Sweetie Face*, Mike Schiffer flying Vlado Lenoch's *Moonbeam McSwine*, and Vlado flying Butch Schroeder's *Lil' Margaret*.

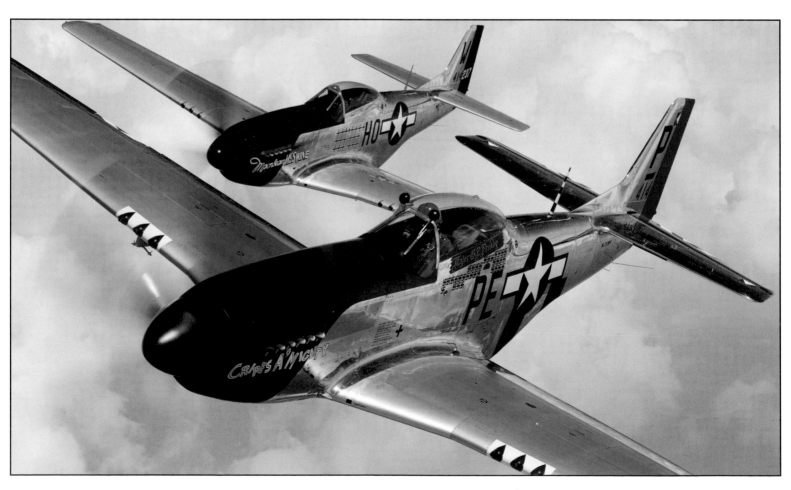

I often refer to the Gathering of Mustangs and Legends because it was a turning point in my career. I started shooting airplanes in 1972 for Cessna. I assisted a commercial photographer who had the Cessna account. For $1.75 an hour, I learned what it meant to be a commercial photographer. A year later, I was shooting for Beech as a free lancer. I shot from my first B-25 in 1976. But, I never appreciated warbirds until 1999 when I attended the Gathering. Since then, warbirds have become my photographic passion. I've learned a lot about their place in history, and I've grown to love their beautiful lines and colorful variations.

During the Gathering, I shot from a B-25 flown by Ed and Connie Bowlin. I also shot with Patty Wagstaff in her Baron, equipped with side windows that opened in flight and a hole in the belly so I could shoot down on top of the subject planes. Since then, we have all become very close friends.

The formations I shot included Pete McManus in his *Petie 3rd*, David Marco in his *Sizzlin' Liz*, and Hank Reichert and Skip Holm in Hank's *Dakota Kid II*. Another flight featured Pete McManus again in *Petie 3rd*, Jimmy Leeward in *Betty Boop*, Tom Wood in his Mustang, and Reg Urschler in *Gunfighter*.

Doug and Jeff Driscoll's *Section Eight* went through a two-year rebuild after an engine failure. I met them at John Lane's facility in Idaho for this photo shoot. It's fun to see a father and his adult son who enjoy each other's friendship so much, and share a common passion for aviation.

If you stay out past sunset at Oshkosh and bring a couple of hand strobes with you, you can get shots like this. Ron Fagen's *Sweet Revenge* is lit by two lights, one with a magenta gel filter over the strobe head, and one with no filtration. Lagging the exposure, or making a long exposure for the overall ambient light, gives the desired effect. It was shot with a Canon EOS 1Ds Digital camera set at 1/15th of a second at f5.0, with the ISO at 100. A tripod helps with these longer exposures.

I first met David Marco during a photo shoot for *Flying Magazine* in 1985. That was before he got his Mustang. It was at the 2002 Sun 'n Fun fly-in where I saw him again. We arranged to shoot these aerials along with Jim Tobul in his Corsair. In many ways, the aviation community is very small. Since 2002, I've shot Jim in the Corsair and flown in his SNJ as the photo platform.

Ron Buccarelli owns and flies this highly modified P-51D racer. It's powered by a Rolls-Royce Griffon engine and has contra-rotating props. *Precious Metal* competes in the Reno Air Races and appears at numerous air shows. I had the opportunity to fly with Ron at Sun 'n Fun, and we climbed above the cloud layer. The sleek canopy, custom tail, and six blades of propeller distinguish this racer from any other Mustang.

Sometimes people ask me if I'm in another airplane when I take these photos! I take a deep breath, smile, and explain the process. This was a challenging shoot, as I'm in another Mustang with Lee Lauderback at the controls while we did formation loops, flying off Eliot Cross in the target ship. We did about 12 loops, in groupings of two, with me switching cameras at the bottom of each first loop. It's very disconcerting looking through the lens and pulling Gs.

OLD CROW AND
GENTLEMAN JIM

3

ROUSH'S MUSTANGS

Jack Roush is one very busy guy.

His business empire now consists of four divisions: Roush Industries, Roush Manufacturing, Roush Performance, and Roush Fenway Racing.

Roush Industries is an engineering and prototype-development company servicing the automotive and transportation industries.

Roush Manufacturing manufactures a wide array of high tech items for home, business, and recreational activities. These vary from computer disc drive components to automotive exterior trim components to aircraft airframe and engine components.

Roush Performance, the first specialty-vehicle company to combine track-proven race technologies with advanced automotive engineering, manufactures high performance road cars and aftermarket performance parts and packages for a number of vehicles including Roush-branded Ford Mustangs and Ford F-150 trucks, and non Roush-branded packages for several other manufacturers.

Roush Racing already held one Winston Cup and one Nextel Cup Championship title in February 2007, when Jack sold half his racing enterprise to John Henry and the Fenway Sports Group, whose holdings include the Boston Red Sox. Now Roush Fenway Racing, with an estimated value in the hundreds of millions of dollars, is NASCAR's most valuable racing powerhouse with more than a dozen entries in three different series.

All together, Jack employs more than 2,000 people operating in 36 facilities in five states plus England, Germany, and Mexico.

Yet he makes time for his deep involvement in the warbird community.

They call Jack "The Cat in the Hat" in NASCAR circles. Look at that hat. See the little Old Glory pin he always wears.

That's were Jack's heart is.

I'm honored to be numbered among his friends.

– Paul Bowen

Nearly everybody is gone now who designed and built the first NA 73X Mustang during those revolutionary 117 days of gestation in 1940. Nearly everybody is gone now who's ever machined and assembled the original parts for the P-51 Mustangs that prototype fighter became, or flew one in combat, or patched up one's battle damage.

But the weapon they created and employed to win the air war over Western Europe in World War II, the amazing P-51 Mustang, still lives a rip roaring life of air shows, air racing, aerobatic exhibitions, and even the occasional friendly furball in the custody and under the stewardship of those of us who take the responsibility so seriously.

Besides being a ton of fun, it's a sacred trust and an honor, and it's a genuine privilege to be a caretaker of the heritage which surrounds it now and for future generations.

Built with an endurance of up to 10 hours, high altitude P-51s performed previously impossible escort missions flying cover for lumbering U.S. bombers in daylight raids deep into Germany. With the first enemy contact of a mission, the Mustangs accelerated to speeds as fast as 505 miles per hour, and their six .50 caliber guns tore huge gashes through the hapless Luftwaffe defenders. Mustang pilots immediately cut U.S. bomber losses, as the bombers pounded Adolph Hitler and his psychopathic dreams of World domination into rubble.

The fortunes of war being what they are, some Mustang mounted warriors achieved more success and notoriety than others. With some regret, it is to the memories and legacies of just a few of so many outstanding fighter pilots, the few lucky and courageous men who so bravely and conspicuously preserved and defended our freedoms, that I gratefully dedicate my time, effort, and financial resources.

My Mustang addiction began in 1993, when I bought my first P-51D Mustang and restored it as the *Old Crow* to honor one of America's bravest heroes, one of the world's greatest aviators, and one of my best friends, Col. Bud Anderson.

During Bud's long aviation career, he logged over 7,000 hours in more than 100 types of aircraft. He became a triple ace in World War II with 16 1/4 kills and completed 116 combat missions in his three trusty *Old Crows* without ever turning back for mechanical reasons or being seriously affected by enemy fire.

My current P-51D is *Gentleman Jim*, which has been restored and painted in remembrance of Bud's good friend Captain Jim Browning. Capt. Browning went missing and was presumed killed in action when his Mustang collided with a Luftwaffe Me 262 jet fighter during a dogfight on February 9, 1945, three months before the German surrender.

Capt. Browning had already become an ace with five kills when he returned to the United States for a break after his first combat tour with the 363rd Fighter Group. Like his friend Bud Anderson, Capt. Browning volunteered to return for a second tour and reported to the 357th Fighter Group out of patriotism and respect. In short order, he scored his next two victories, and then a third. Including his last, a mid-air collision with the first German Jet, he finished up with nine confirmed kills to his credit. Russian prisoners who searched *Gentleman Jim's* wreckage afterward

brought their German captors a gold ring and some currency, Capt. Browning's identification tag, and a photograph with his name on it, but his body was never recovered. For that reason, Capt. James Browning is still listed on The Wall of the Missing at the American Military Cemetery in Luxembourg.

I'm pleased to report, through the efforts of many *Gentleman Jim* is a first rate Mustang restoration a real hotrod in the sky and pleasure to fly. It's a humble but fitting tribute to Capt. Browning, a brave and skilled warrior who gave his all.

Now my next P-51 is nearly ready, and I am very excited as I anticipate its arrival. Under restoration for nearly a decade, this one is becoming the earlier and extremely rare "razorback" B model. It represents the historic first pairing in April, 1942 of the Mustang's tough, elegant, maneuverable airframe with the Packard-built, Rolls-Royce designed, two-stage, super-charged Merlin 1650 V-12 engine. In contrast to the Mustang's original supercharged Allison 1710 V-12 engine's poor performance above 15,000 feet, Rolls-Royce's new Packard-licensed-and-built Merlin drove the Mustang to the astonishing speed of more than 440 miles per hour in level flight at 25,000 feet, and could take it all the way up to an absolute ceiling of more than 40,000 feet.

I sold my first P 51D, *Old Crow*, a while back, so I'm having my new P-51B restored as Col. Anderson's second P-51B model, which was fitted with a Spitfire canopy called Sir Malcolm's Hood. I've chosen this particular restoration partly because I miss having an *Old Crow* around; and, after all, it was Bud Anderson's favorite.

Besides, Bud is a lot more than a hero.

He's a dear friend.

– Jack Roush

Jack Roush and close friend Ed Bowlin, have fun during the annual Experimental Aircraft Association's AirVenture at Oshkosh, Wisconsin. They have flown together for years and have complete trust in each others' abilities and judgement.

Both of these planes are P-51D models. Jack's latest restoration, completed in September, 2007, is a P-51B with the *Old Crow* markings.

This D model *Old Crow* was sold to Jim Hagedorn in 2006. Pages 90 and 91 feature Jim flying outstanding formation on the tail of the B-25. He asked me during the briefing if I could get some head-on shots of him. I'd never flown with him before, so I replied, "If you can put it where I need it, I'll get the shot." Well, obviously, I got the shot!

Triple Ace Bud Anderson flew *Old Crow* in 2003, forming up on the B-25 *Georgia Mae*. Some of these images were taken from the open escape hatch, aft of the wing. Others were shot from the open tail-gunner's position. It's amazing to me that at Bud's mature age he doesn't appear to have lost any of his flying finesse. What an honor to call him and his wife Ellie, Gail's and my friends.

In February, 2004, I had the rare privilege to ride along in Jack Roush's CitationJet, with Dave Zantop in the left seat, and Connie Bowlin in the right. The objective was to capture Jack's Mustangs while they created contrails. We started the morning at 4:15 a.m. to get into position when the sun rose. After requesting a block of airspace from 26,000 to 31,000 feet, we found contrails at 27,000. A haze layer made us ask for 35,000, and up we went. The flight went beautifully, and for once I was warm during a winter shoot, inside the comfy CJ while it was -56°F outside!

CORSAIRS

CORSAIR FOREWORD
BY DALE SNODGRASS

Thanks in large part to his father, who was a Marine Aviator in World War II and then a test pilot for Convair, Sperry, and Grumman, my buddy, Dale "Snort" Snodgrass, has been working around airplanes and flying since he learned how to walk.

With an early and burning desire to fly carrier-based fighters, Dale earned his private pilot's license in the Navy ROTC flight program during his junior year at the University of Minnesota. Then, after graduation, he went on to a long, distinguished career flying F-14 Tomcats.

Dale kicked off his Naval career by becoming first just-out-of-flight-school graduate ever selected for F-14 training *and* the first non fleet-experienced ensign ever to "trap" a Tomcat on a carrier deck – feats he immediately followed up with day and night carrier landing qualifications. As one of the Navy's elite *Top Gun* graduates, in 1985, Dale became the *Fighter Pilot of the Year*, and in 1986, he was selected as the Navy's *Best F-14 Pilot* and Grumman Aerospace's *Topcat of the Year*.

He also got into some typically fighter pilot-style hot water with his commander for a super low-level departure he made from Rota, Spain. Aggressiveness is essential for fighter pilots, so all was forgiven – eventually – and Dale continued to fly the F-14 right to the edge of its limitations.

During his 24 years of operational fighter squadron and wing tours, Dale flew combat operations in Libya, led 34 combat missions during Operation Desert Storm, and still stands as the high-time F-14 pilot with more than 4,800 hours and over 1,200 carrier takeoffs and landings. Characteristically leading from the front, as squadron commander, he told his aircrews, "Only three things count: fighting the Tomcats better than anyone else; landing on the carrier better than anyone else; and having the best maintained aircraft." His squadron won every award available, and Dale rose to command all the Navy's F-14 Tomcats as Commander Fighter Wing Atlantic.

These days, you can find him doing what he does best – flying fighters as they should be flown, not operationally or in combat, but as a marquis air show performer.

Oh, and let me mention this – he's a terrific Corsair pilot – and a fellow surfer too!

– Paul Bowen

Designed in 1938 to meet a Navy requirement for a carrier-based aircraft with performance to match the best land and carrier-based fighters of the day, the Corsair is one of the most readily identifiable aircraft in the world.

It was a challenge to meet the Navy's order. Carrier-based aircraft have to be overbuilt and heavier than ground-based aircraft so they can stand up to the stress of deck landings, which makes equal performance really hard to achieve – and yet Vought did it. Powered by the Pratt & Whitney R-2800 Double Wasp radial engine, the Corsair prototype took to the skies on May 29, 1940, and within a short time became the first U.S. single-production aircraft capable of 400 miles per hour in level flight.

Built for a real slugfest, Corsairs came into service in 1942 with six .50-caliber Brownings loaded with 2,300 rounds of ammunition. That gave Corsair pilots a solid minute's worth of withering firepower. The Corsair was a better plane than the F4F-3 and F4F-4 Wildcats the Navy was using at the time, and it was superior in some ways to the F6F Hellcat, which replaced the Wildcat. But more important than that, it was faster and could out-climb and out-dive the primary Japanese fighter, the Mitsubishi A6M Zero. Thanks to its robust superiority and the Navy's better training and tactics, end-of-the-war tallies show an 11:1 kill ratio for the Corsair of 2,140 air-combat victories to 189 losses to enemy aircraft.

Still, the Corsair has its quirks.

At low speeds, it loses lift on the port wing and drops that side before the starboard, which can surprise you at the wrong moment. That long "hose nose" accommodates a huge fuel tank behind the engine, but it blocks your view when you're taxiing and during the last critical seconds of a carrier landing. The landing gear is maybe a little too springy, and if you land too slow, you can find yourself bouncing high in a ton of airplane with no lift – especially on the left wing – and you'll be in for a real exciting touchdown.

That and a few other characteristics make the Corsair a seasoned pilot's airplane and contributed to one of its many nicknames, the "ensign eliminator." In fact, 922 Corsairs were destroyed in accidents during World War II, nearly five times as many as the Japanese shot down.

On the other hand, the ground troops nicknamed the Corsair, "Sweetheart," for its ability to destroy the enemy with its .50-caliber or 20-millimeter guns and napalm, 2,000 pounds of bombs, or four 5-inch rockets. On the receiving end, the Japanese nicknamed it "Whistling Death," Whistling for the sound its turbocharged engine made and Death, well that speaks for itself. Nothing humorous about that, is there?

Which brings up an interesting point. A while back somebody asked me if I could remember any humorous moments while I was flying. No. Don't get me wrong. I'm anything but dour. I have a good sense of humor, and I can tell lots of funny stories about myself and my friends – but they all took place on the ground.

In contrast, the cockpit is an unforgiving place fit only for the most focused of people. Focus or die. Adding to the seriousness of the environment, you're flying a heavy machine moving very fast, so if you lose concentration, if you mess up and die, you might take somebody else with you.

But just because flying isn't funny doesn't mean it's not fun – because it is. It's been fun for me my whole life, and it's the only work in the world I've ever wanted to do. And these photography shoots with Paul Bowen are great fun.

When I work with Paul, I get to fly amazing, beautifully restored World War II and Korean Fighters in formation with a B-25 photo ship. I get to work with professional aviators and the world's most professional aviation photographer – capturing history and creating art. Everything about that is fun. And because it's aviation, everything about that is serious as well.

It's a demanding kind of flying, putting all those fast-moving parts in such close proximity, and it has to work with machinelike precision. That's where experience really pays off for the aircrews, the photographer, and finally for you, the reader who will see what we've accomplished.

Well our photographer is absolutely the best. Paul has been doing photography shoots like this for more than 30 years. His experience helps us pilots keep everything safe and enables us to position these "flying sculptures," as Paul appropriately calls the aircraft, for the best shots with the best backgrounds and then fly home to be dazzled by the pictures we've helped create. Paul always thanks the pilots when we've finished one of these shoots. Well, now it's my turn.

Paul, thank you for making all this work we do in the air look magical when framed and hanging on the wall – and of coarse when we open the cover to one of your books. It's a true privilege and honor to share the skies with the Topgun of Air to Air Photography.

– Captain Dale "Snort" Snodgrass USN (Ret)

The distinctive inverted gull-wing design of the Corsair makes it one of the most beautiful and easily recognized fighters of World War II. The wing design was initially a practical solution to a problem. To take advantage of the powerful engine, a huge, 13-foot diameter propeller was used. But for adequate prop clearance, a conventional wing would need tall, spindly landing gear, unusable for carrier landings. The gull-wing was the solution.

The Corsair actually started its career as a land-based fighter assigned to the Marines in the Pacific. It immediately proved more than a match for the Japanese Zero. The Corsair was maneuverable with an exceptional roll rate, and it was the first single-seat fighter to exceed 400 mph in level flight. The Japanese nicknamed it "Whistling Death" because of the sound of the airflow over the leading edge oil coolers.

The Air Museum Planes of Fame's F4U-1A is the oldest flying Corsair. Built by Vought in 1943, it spent time in San Diego before being shipped to active service in the Pacific. After the war, it was bought by Twentieth Century Fox Studios as a movie prop. It sat in the background, missing an engine, engine cowling and tail surfaces. The museum restored the plane to flying condition in 1976. Since then, it has appeared in numerous air shows and has flown in Hollywood productions, including the "Baa Baa Blacksheep" television series, which centered around Marine Major "Pappy" Boyington and his rowdy squadron.

This Corsair has been painted with two different paint schemes. The one on the left was replaced in 2003 by the tri-color scheme shown below. Note that the earlier models were fitted with a three-bladed prop, which was replaced by four blades in the later models.

These photos were taken from the open canopy of a North American T-6 trainer. I was seated behind the pilot, Mark Foster. While in flight, I slid open the canopy and swiveled my seat to face aft. I had to be careful not to sit up too high or lean my lens into the slip-stream. I directed Mark's heading and altitude over our headset/intercom connection. He would then relay my specific positions for the targets to move to. We're constantly moving the target ships as a flight or individually within the flight.

I contacted my friends at the Planes of Fame, and asked if they would put up a Mustang and Corsair for me to shoot and place on the cover of this book. They did, and we got what we needed. My wife, Gail, is seated behind John Hinton, in his brother Steve's Mustang, following Kevin Eldridge in the Corsair. Kevin has the distinction of having bailed out of a burning Corsair during an air show in 1994. With the plane engulfed in flames, Kevin jumped hitting the horizontal stabilizer and breaking his neck and leg before opening his chute and floating to safety.

On another occasion, the Planes of Fame Corsair went airborne with Ray Dieckman's *Marine's Dream*. Ray personally worked on his plane's restoration, earning him Reserve Grand Champion at Oshkosh 2000. He also received a trophy for The Golden Wrench Award, acknowledging all the work he'd put in during the five-year restoration. It's rare to see an owner do his own work with such stunning results.

Marine's Dream was built by Goodyear, and is designated as an FG-1D Corsair. Under an agreement with Chance Vought, Goodyear and Brewster produced Corsairs. Vought made 4,699 units, Goodyear 4,006 and Brewster, 735. Goodyear's FG-1D was the same aircraft as the Vought F4U-1.

Note the external fuel tanks on *Marine's Dream*. They could be jettisoned when the enemy was encountered and a dog fight ensued.

Jim Read, president of the Indiana Aviation Museum, owns and flies this beautiful F4U-5N Corsair. It was built in 1947 and served two years in the Navy before being put in storage and shipped off to Honduras under the Military Assistance Program. It was brought back to the United States by a private individual in 1978. After it passed through several owners, Read purchased it in 1998.

Read and Dale "Snort" Snodgrass fly the Corsair at air shows throughout the country each year. These next pages show both pilots behind the controls.

The Collings Foundation is dedicated to preserving the machines that built world aviation history. They are well known for their annual Wings of Freedom Tour, taking their B-17; B-24, which is the world's only flying B-24; and B-25 to airports around the United States. For a small fee, people can tour the planes on the ground. There is also the opportunity to take a 30 minute flight in any of the three planes.

Along with the bombers, they have a pristine F4U-5NL Corsair, but it has had some bad luck over the years. After an involved restoration which began in 1993, it crashed in 1997 into the Atlantic Ocean due to engine failure caused by contaminated fuel. The Corsair was rebuilt again, and in September, 2003, a gear problem forced Dale Snodgrass to belly land. Finally, in 2004, the Corsair was awarded Grand Champion Post World War II at AirVenture in Oshkosh. Dale Snodgrass flew it for me at Sun 'n Fun in 2004.

The bulbous pod on the right wing was an Air Intercept Radar Radome. The Navy was interested in a night interceptor, and such pods were added to 34 airplanes.

Max Chapman, Jr.'s Marine trainer sports a unique paint scheme. Having served as a Marine, Max chose to honor his branch of service with this airplane, which was in the Korean War aboard the USS Boxer. It was also seen in the television series, "Baa Baa Black Sheep."

Max bought the plane in 1998 and had it restored. In 2000, he won Reserve Grand Champion Post World War II at AirVenture, Oshkosh. At the same event, he won Grand Champion World War II with one of his Mustangs. When Max does something, he does it right.

In 1963 during his sophomore year at UNC in the final seconds of a crucial game, Max kicked the winning field goal, leading the TarHeels to victory over Duke, and a spot in the Gator Bowl. Life is intense for Max. I love his spirit of going all-out.

These photos were taken over Lake Winnebago, Wisconsin, with Ray Dieckman at the controls. Warbird enthusiast Tony Raftis had just purchased the plane and wanted some aerials. Tony has amassed an impressive group of planes over the past few years, and has developed a niche market with his Provenance Fighter Sales.

In June of 2005, five Corsairs descended upon Bridgeport, Connecticut, the home of the Chance Vought Company which designed and built the Corsair. "Corsairs over Connecticut" was a great success, honoring the people who designed, built, maintained, and flew the planes.

Rob Collings flew The Collings Foundation's F4U-5NL and Tom Duffy piloted his new acquisition, the FG-1D, *Marine's Dream*. The 25,000 people who attended the weekend gathering were treated to close-up inspection of the airplanes.

Jim Vocell flew the American Airpower Museum's FG-1D *Skyboss*, Gerry Beck flew his F4U-4, and Dave Morss flew the Fighter Factory's FG-1D in formation for my camera perched in the tail of Larry Kelley's B-25 *Panchito*.

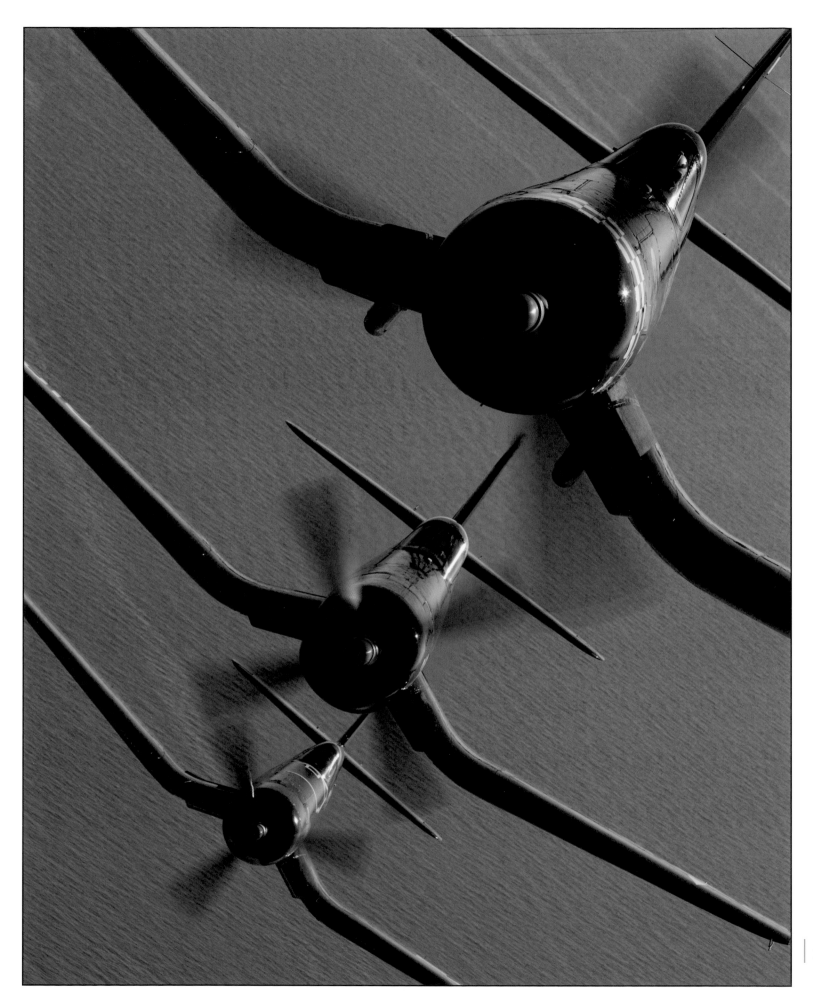

Jerry Yagen's Fighter Factory is amassing a wonderful collection of beautifully restored airplanes, including a Curtiss P-40E Kittyhawk, Vickers Supermarine Mark IX Spitfire, P-51D Mustang, Hurricane MkXII, FG-1D Corsair, TBM Avenger, PBY Catalina, Polikarpov I-15*bis,* and AD-4 Skyraider. The Fighter Factory is not a museum but a private collection, which is a part of the Aircraft Discovery Division of Aviation Institute of Maintenance located in Norfolk, Virginia. Their motto is "Preserving History Through the Recovery and Restoration of World War II Aircraft."

I've photographed Jerry while he piloted different planes from his collection, but on this occasion, Dave Morss was behind the controls. I've also shot Dave on other flights, so I knew I was flying with a pro. Dave is a test pilot, air racer, flight instructor and warbird pilot. He was the test pilot for the first flights on 35 different prototype aircraft. He has competed in more races than anyone in the history of Reno Air Racing, and he flies warbirds whenever possible.

Jim Tobul and his father Joe flew this Corsair until November 10, 2002. On that day, rather than bailing out and taking a chance the airplane would injure someone on the ground, Joe guided his crippled airplane away from a populated area and courageously crashed into a swamp and died.

I'd only flown once with Joe, and that was at a Gathering of Corsairs in September 2002, just two months before his death. I've spent more time with his son, Jim, and have flown with Jim in the target ship and as the photo platform pilot, in his SNJ with the canopy open. These pictures are of Jim in the cockpit.

This Corsair resides in Brazil at the *Museu Asas De Um Sonho – Wings of a Dream Museum*. My late friend, Comandante Rolim Adolfo Amaro, founder and CEO of TAM Airlines, started collecting planes for his museum many years before he died in a helicopter accident in 2001. Today the museum, which is located near São Paulo at the São Carlos airport, houses over 60 pristine planes, most of which are airworthy, including this F4U-1.

The Royal New Zealand Air Force operated 424 Corsairs, including this one. After the War it ended up in Provo, Utah, where it was discovered in a junkyard in 1965. In 1967, it was purchased by an individual who had it restored into flying condition by 1981. It crashed in 1983, and after another six year restoration, it flew again. In 1999, it was donated to the TAM collection. Rolim's brother, João Francisco Amaro, was instrumental in developing the collection and is the president of the museum.

The Lone Star Flight Museum, located in Galveston, Texas, has one of the finest collections of flying warbirds in the world. I've shot from the museum's B-25 on numerous commercial assignments, but my first opportunity to shoot its Corsair came at Oshkosh, with Doug Rozendaal behind the controls. Doug and I have flown a lot together, often with him at the controls of the B-25 platform.

It can be difficult flying close behind the B-25. The wake turbulence wants to "spit out" the trailing plane. There's a lot of "dirty air" coming off the B-25, and it takes experience to know how to avoid it or react to it as it affects the flying characteristics of the target. In the shot below, Rozendaal came in so close that I had to use a wide-angle lens to get the entire plane in my frame. He's stepped down just below the "wash," in smooth air.

In September, 2002, Corsair enthusiast Mint Moore III, arranged the Gathering of Corsairs and Legends at the Mount Comfort Airport in Indiana. His goal was to assemble Corsair pilots, crew and factory workers, along with as many Corsairs as could attend the weekend celebration.

Seven Corsairs attended the event. I shot them on the ground and air-to-air from the B-25 *Pacific Princess* flown by Carl Scholl and Tony Ritzman from Aero Traders in Chino, California. In attendance were Gerry Beck flying his F4U-4, Steve Bakke piloting Ray Thompson's F4U-5NL, Joe and Jim Tobul in their F4U-4, Jim Read and Dale Snodgrass flying Jim's F4U-5, John Muszala in Max Chapman, Jr.'s F4U-4, Mike George piloting his F4U-5NL, and Ray Dieckman in his FG-1D, *Marine's Dream*.

The image to the right shows Mike George flying the "inside turn", with him at the 7:00 position of the B-25. With both planes flying left-hand orbits, and placing Mike slightly high, I get a "power shot" as we continue our turn. A standard rate turn is completed in two minutes, no matter what speed you're flying. So I get a variety of lighting and angles as I direct the target up and down, forward and backward, and to its left or right.

The aerial portion of this shoot was extra fun for me. The Corsair, with its unique construction, makes a wonderful target for my camera. One Corsair is great to shoot, but more than one makes it even more fun.

The shot on the right shows Jim Tobul, John Muszala and Dale "Snort" Snodgrass stepped down below the tail of the B-25. This may not be a normal formation position, but it looked great to the camera. These guys are outstanding formation pilots. I'd flown with each of them before and knew how good they were. Plus, all three had been friends of mine for some time and that adds a personal touch to this shot. During the shoot, it helps my creative juices to flow knowing that I will be sharing these images with them later. We all put out extra effort during this sequence.

On the following pages you'll see several flights of three and five planes. The more planes you add to the formation, the more difficult the flying and shooting. My compliments go to Jim and Joe Tobul, John Muszala, Dale "Snort" Snodgrass, Jim Read, Steve Bakke, Gerry Beck, Mike George, and Ray Dieckman.

Gary Kohs' AirVenture Grand Champion FG-1D Corsair was one of over 4,000 versions of the Vought designed airplane to be built at Goodyear's Akron, Ohio, plant during World War II. The success of the restoration was due to the work of John and Nancy Lane at their shop in Idaho. Airpower Unlimited's crew spent over 17,000 man-hours during thirteen years completing the plane.

In June, 2004, a reunion brought production workers and test pilots to the Military Aviation Preservation Society's "Corsair Homecoming" during their annual MAPS air show. Center of attention went to Kohs' Corsair.

John Lane attended the ceremony and flew the plane while I shot from Larry Kelley's *Panchito*. For me, the highlight of the weekend was seeing the workers who had built the Corsairs come up to the plane and inspect the areas they had constructed decades before.

Over the years, Charles Osborn, Jr., has put his money where his passion is – in restoring World War II fighters. His Vintage Fighters restoration shop in Sellersburg, Indiana, recently completed this beautiful Corsair.

I flew with Duane Carroll in Dave Holmes' T-6 to meet up with Brad Hood and his crew to shoot ground shots and aerials of the plane. Not unlike other in-depth restorations, this project took years to complete at a substantial cost – but the results were worth it. After my ground shots were taken, we headed for some sunset aerials with Brad in tow. The results of the shoot show off the beauty of the Corsair as flown by one of the best pilots in the business.

As is common within the warbird community, airplanes change hands. In 2007, Rod Lewis added this Corsair to his growing fleet of museum-quality planes. It's comforting to see warbird collectors amass inventories of planes and give them the attention they need to remain in flight. May these flying sculptures be a reminder of the pilots who gave all they could to preserve the freedoms we enjoy today.

F2G-1D Super Corsair

F2G-1D SUPER CORSAIR
BY BOB ODEGAARD

Captain Bob Odegaard is among the world's very best warbird rebuilders.

In addition to keeping busy with restorations, Captain Bob's company, Odegaard Aviation in Kindred, North Dakota, operates several warbirds including his Goodyear F2G-1D *Super Corsair*, featured in this section, his North American P-51D Mustang, *Dazzling Donna*, which appeared on pages 64-67, and his famous, all-yellow Douglas C-47 Skytrain with the smiley face, *Duggy*; plus, among others, an F6F Hellcat, a P-40 Warhawk, a Yak 3, and a T-28 Trojan.

Born on a North Dakota farm seven miles from the airport where he works, Captain Bob has been flying for 45 years including 31 years of crop dusting – over 18,000 hours so far. His pilot's license bears a no longer-issued endorsement granting him the heady privilege of flying "all makes and models of single and multiengine powered authorized aircraft;" and he's flown just about everything that leaves the ground including gliders, seaplanes, helicopters, and jets.

Bob is a good guy, generous with his time and careful in his work, and I love flying with him and taking pictures of him and his warbirds.

As I've aged I've come to appreciate how precious time is. My family is very important to me and I know Bob's is to him. But he does find time to give to others outside of his family. His dedication to the *Duggy* project is the perfect example of his giving spirit.

And people wonder what he does in his spare time? Well, for one thing, he is a co-producer in the feature film *Thunder Over Reno*, which was released in the fall of 2007. His Corsair is also the *star*, which makes Bob the "behind-the-scenes" star. The action in the movie is compelling, the photography stunning, and the flying, spectacular. What else would you expect from Odegaard!

– Paul Bowen

Look at this!

You'll never see another one.

It is unique.

This is the Goodyear F2G-1D Super Corsair No. 57, the very airplane that won the 1949 Cleveland Air Races Tinnerman Trophy Race and took third place in the 1949 Cleveland Air Races Thompson Trophy Race.

After World War II, lots of Corsairs went on the surplus market, and No. 57 was one of them. Cook Cleland bought it for around $1,500 in 1949, and it joined two other FG2s he then owned. He turned it over to Ben McKillen to prepare it for the national air races, and the only special preparation McKillen made to it was the paint job.

The last time the Super Corsair flew in those days was in the summer of 1950, when Cleland took it up and did aerobatics in it for an air show at Euclid Road Airport in Willoughby, Ohio. After that, it pretty much disappeared, passing through a few owners' hands and some halfhearted restoration starts for 45 years.

In 1995, I found it, bought it, and brought it to my shop in Kindred, North Dakota. We restored it to its original racing colors, the ones McKillen had selected back in 1949 – with one of its four propeller blades painted white and the other three black to give the illusion of the propeller turning slowly – and in 1999, the Super Corsair won the Rolls-Royce Aviation Heritage International.

Here at Odegard Aviation, we're proud of this one, and we're proud of all the work we do.

Now, all Corsairs were built for speed. Though the primary Japanese fighter, the Mitsubishi A6M Zero, could easily turn inside the Corsair at low speeds, the basic-issue Corsair was faster, more heavily armed, and could out-climb and out-dive the enemy fighter. Additionally, in a gunfight the Corsair could take severe punishment and keep flying, in contrast to the comparatively fragile Zero, which had little armor and was without self-sealing fuel tanks.

By avoiding the slow fight and capitalizing on the Corsair's speed, Navy and Marine pilots found it relatively simple to place enemy aircraft in their six .50-caliber Browning machine guns' killing zone and keep them there long enough to inflict major damage.

But then, toward the end of the war as Japan became more desperate and sought a way to delay the invasion they expected, the Navy encountered a new weapon, a real surprise. The Kamikaze. Under heavy fighter escort, Japanese suicide pilots in explosive-laden Zeros would approach their targets at high altitudes and nose over in steep, single-minded dives. No fighter in the Navy could climb fast enough from a carrier deck to fight through the Zero escorts and head off the Kamikazes before they tore into the fleet. So the Navy placed an order for a fighter capable of climbing rapidly to high altitude and attacking the suicide aircraft before they could begin their diving attacks.

Goodyear Aircraft Company took up the challenge and built ten F2G Super Corsairs, the F2G-1s and their sister models the F2G-2s, around Pratt & Whitney Wasp Major 28-cylinder R-4360-4, four-row "corncob" radial engines. This new, larger engine could develop 3,500 horsepower for takeoff – rather than the 2,100 to 2,450 horsepower the 18-cylinder Pratt & Whitney Double Wasp R-2800 variants powering the Navy's standard Corsairs generated. All built with new, teardrop canopies to increase the pilots' all-around visibility, the F2G-1 Super Corsairs, like this one, were designed and built for land-based operations while the -2 models were for carrier use.

If it had made it into combat, this Super Corsair could have done the Navy's job. It'll fly at 450 miles per hour at 25,000 feet, and its service ceiling is 38,000 feet. Fortunately of course, when Army Air Corps B-29s dropped atomic bombs on Hiroshima

Bob uses his C-47, *Duggy – The Smile in the Sky*, to reach young people as he attends airshows and promotes positive character building traits: "Know good from bad, right from wrong, respect others and chase your dream!"

and Nagasaki, the United States put an abrupt end to World War II in the Pacific – before any F2G model Super Corsairs were ready for combat.

The Navy no longer needed a Kamikaze killer, problems had begun to emerge with the F2G models, and the jet age was upon us. The Navy abandoned the project.

And all these great warbirds in this book would have been abandoned too without the efforts, investments, and, yes, the love of the people who have found them and restored them.

Now the best thing about getting to work with Paul Bowen is, well, getting to work with Paul Bowen. He runs a professional photography shoot, he gets the pictures quickly and precisely, he keeps everybody safe – and he keeps everybody happy. He's just a tremendously nice guy with a camera, a razor-sharp eye, and trip-hammer reflexes.

And as for all his photographs in this book, I'll say just what I said when I started this introduction for the Super Corsair chapter.

Look at this!

–Bob Odegaard

The Goodyear Aircraft Company built 10 F2G Super Corsairs at the end of World War II. Bob Odegaard's is the only one flying today. In 1949, painted as you see it today, and sporting the number 57, it won the Tinnerman Trophy at the Cleveland Air Races. In 1995, Bob found the derelict airplane, spent four years restoring number 57, and flies it at air shows, at the Reno Air Races and for movies. Bob's restoration facilities in Kindred, North Dakota, focus primarily on Corsairs and Mustangs.

This was a fun shoot. I'd been in North Dakota with Tim Savage, publisher of *Warbird Digest*, shooting Mustangs for the magazine. Bob agreed to fly both his Mustang and Super Corsair for me as I shot from Tim's B-25. I'd seen the Super Corsair perform at various air shows, and had shot Bob in his DC-3 *Duggy*. *Duggy* is painted bright yellow to draw attention as it tours the U.S. with the message, "dreams do come true," as it helps young people discover the world of flight. That shoot had gone very well, and I knew I was in for a treat with Bob flying nimble fighters.

After briefing, we departed with Bob in *Dazzling Donna*, his P-51D. There was a scattered cloud layer at about 6,000 feet, directly above his private airstrip. We worked our way on top and flew for about 30 minutes. The B-25 continued circling above his airport while he safely dove between the clouds and landed only to return minutes later in the Corsair. This was a new kind of "happy hour" for me. We continued to shoot until nearly sunset as Bob put number 57 through its paces. I went home a happy camper after my private air show.

As the sun sank lower, the texture of the clouds increased. I try to keep my images simple and clean, showing the airplane in a banking angle to capture the feeling of movement, and always trying to photograph it against an interesting background, one which doesn't detract from the subject. The bright red and white paint scheme helped it "pop" from almost any background.

I shoot mostly from the open tail-gunner's position when using the B-25 as my photo platform. But, sometimes I'll crawl over the bomb bay, through the tunnel under the pilots, and into the nose where another gunner would have shot something other than a Canon. By wearing black light-weight gloves and a dark jacket, and draping black cloths from the structural supports, I can shoot through the glass with minimal reflections. The most dangerous part of this 3/4 rear shooting is the lead change. It's critical that the change of lead is communicated clearly between pilots. Once the lead change has occurred, I direct both planes – their headings, bank angles, and altitude.

Prior to sunset, I headed back to the tail. Bob Odegaard is such a good pilot that I started to run out of ideas to get more variety in our shots. We were killing about 15 minutes until the sun got lower, when I asked him to start at the 7:00 position and fly past our tail on knife-edge, ending up around our 5:00. Without hesitation, he swept across my field of view. I fine-tuned my request and he banked past me another time. I love it when a plan works.

We wrapped up the shoot working the clouds to achieve my signature "vortices" shots. This evening was the first time I recorded vortices created by a warbird. They are always there, created by the wings, but are only revealed when there's smoke or a weather phenomenon, such as clouds or fog.

PILOTS, PANELS & DETAILS

Panels & Details

Very few of us get the opportunity to climb into the cockpit of a warbird. During the past few years, the owners and pilots of these planes have allowed me free access to their treasures. Because I'm not a pilot, I can't fully appreciate the subtle differences between the panels. But, I can enjoy the visual variations I saw within the different airplanes.

Some owners have restored their airplanes with as much authenticity and originality as possible, while others have chosen to add modern equipment for easier, safer operation.

These next four pages display Mustang cockpits and details.

P-51C - *Ina the Macon Belle* - Kermit Weeks

P-51A - *Mrs. Virginia* - The Air Museum - Planes of Fame

TF-51 - *Kentucky Babe* - Dick Thurman

P-51D - *Cripes A' Mighty* - Ken Wagnon

P-51C - *Betty Jane* - Max Chapman, Jr.

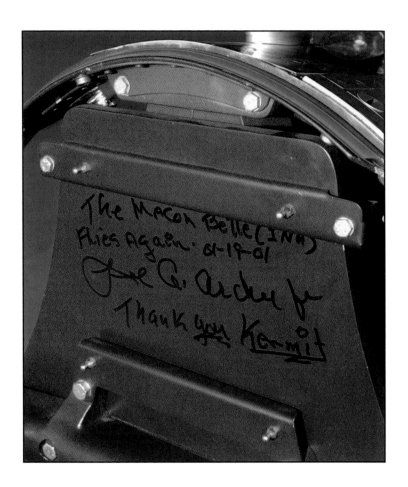

The Macon Belle (INH)
Flies Again - 01-19-01
Lee A. Archer Jr
Thank you Kermit

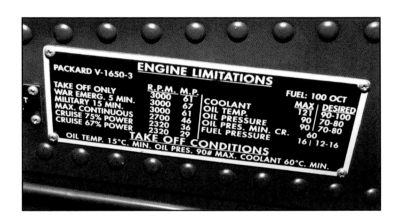

The Corsair's cockpit was designed very differently from the Mustang's. The overall shape and arrangement of the instruments is dramatically different.

The oldest flying Corsair, pictured below, is owned and flown by The Air Museum Planes of Fame. This simple, straight forward panel displays the basics needed and available when the Corsair was introduced. The complexity of the Collings Foundation panel shows what became available.

FG-1D - Ray Dieckman

F4U-1A - The Air Museum - Planes of Fame

FG-1D - Rod Lewis

F4U-5NL - Lone Star Flight Museum

F4U-5NL - Collings Foundation

MUSTANG PILOTS

The pilots are the heroes of this book. I have been very fortunate to have flown with some of the world's best warbird pilots and even more fortunate to count many of them as close friends.

Flying formation is not easy. You first need to be a competent pilot, then you need specific training and practice to become proficient and safe at it.

Most of these Mustang pilots fly other warbirds, too, but if you ask Mustang pilots what their favorite airplanes to fly are, they usually just smile, and if they're within distance, just pat the P-51 on the cowling and continue smiling.

Mustang pilots gather at Oshkosh: Standing: Gen. Reg Urschler, Tony Buechler, Dick James (who we lost on July 26, 2005), Jeff Williams, and Jack Roush.
Kneeling: Chuck Greenhill, Vlado Lenoch, Jim Read, and Ron Fagen.

Robbie Patterson

Mike DeMarino

John Hinton, John Maloney, Kevin Eldridge and Steve Hinton
from The Air Museum - Planes of Fame, Chino, California

John Hinton

Steve Hinton

Kevin Eldridge

John Maloney

Kermit Weeks

Eric Huppert, Ed Shipley, Max Chapman, Jr., and Lee Lauderback

Eliot Cross

Ed Shipley and Lee Lauderback

Bob Tullius

Alan Anderson

Ed and Connie Bowlin

C.E. "Bud" Anderson

Jack Roush and Ed Bowlin

Jim Hagedorn and Jack Roush

David Marco

Jimmy Leeward

Doug Rozendaal

Jim Tobul and Don Hinz briefing before a flight at Kitty Hawk, 12-16-2003

Noble Peterson and Hank Reichert

Ken Dahlberg and Paul Ehlen

Gerald Beck

Bob Odegaard

Bev and Chuck Greenhill

Aubrey Hair

Rod Lewis

Mark Huffstutler

Todd Stuart

Fred Cabanas

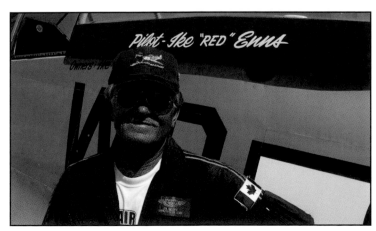

Ike Enns

Ron Fagen

Mike Schiffer

Al Schiffer

Vlado Lenoch

Tom Patten

John Lane and Butch Schroeder

Jeff Driscoll, Doug Driscoll and John Lane

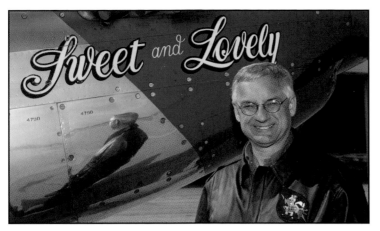

Bob Baker

Ron Buccarelli

Dick James

Tom Wood - Photo: Paul Newman

Doug Fisher and Nathan Davis

Pete McManus

CORSAIR PILOTS

At the good-natured risk of offending both groups, Mustang and Corsair pilots, by putting them together in one book, I know most pilots and the general public agree both these aircraft are the most beautiful and popular of all the American World War II fighters.

The history and emotions reflected in images of the Corsair move the hearts of people who know its background. The sheer beauty and power of the images themselves move the hearts of everyone.

Gerald Beck

Jim Vocell

Dave Morss

Joe Tobul directs the pilot briefing at the Gathering of Corsairs and Legends, which was held in September, 2002, just two months before Joe was killed flying his Corsair.

Jim Tobul

Bob Odegaard

John Lane

Brad Hood

Steve Bakke

Mike George

Dale "Snort" Snodgrass

Jim Read

Doug Rozendaal

John Muszala

Kevin Eldridge

Mike DeMarino

Ray Dieckman

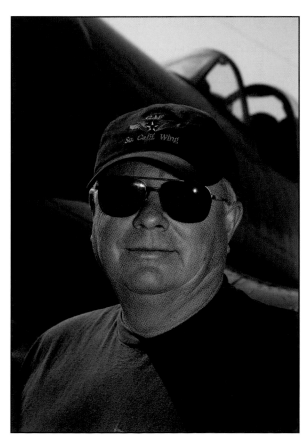

Steve Barber

Rita Reutter - a.k.a. Rosie the Riveter

GALLERY

KITTY HAWK CENTENNIAL

What else can be said about Kitty Hawk?

In December, 2003, aviation friends from around the world descended upon North Carolina for The Centennial Celebration. There is always a sense that you're standing on sacred ground at Kitty Hawk, but this was different.

The famous and not-yet-famous shared their enthusiasm and love for aviation as they braved rains and bitter cold windchill.

Paul and Gail shared the Celebration with close friends Dr. Michael and Patti Schloss, and Dr. Bill and Charlotte Harrison. Sadly, Patti passed away the following month.

Dr. Bill and Charlotte Harrison appear prepared for anything.

Dr. Michael and Patti Schloss seek shelter from the challenging weather.

Skip Lehman organized the Centenial Event and is involved in all aspects of promoting aviation.

Everyone was drenched at the Event – but everyone was smiling.

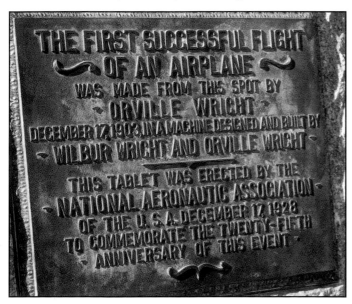

The Centennial Celebration was a reunion of those who had a passion for aviation and wanted to share it with their friends. Gail and Paul have made so many friends through flying. There's a quality of character that seems to permeate aviation. One of their favorite aviation personalities and friends is the legendary pilot Bob Hoover. They were honored to have Bob write the foreword to their last book, *Air To Air Warbirds*. Bob flew most of the models of planes featured in *Warbirds*, and has been decorated by both the civilian and military communities.

Senator and Mrs. John Glenn were great company at the pre-Centennial banquet hosted by the Experimental Aircraft Association.

Paul and Gail share a festive moment with Charlotte and Dr. Bill Harrison. Bill is Paul's warbird mentor.

The Celebration was a wonderful time of reunion with friends like Ed and Connie Bowlin. Ed and Connie, both retired Delta Captains, are very active with EAA and the warbird community.

John and Martha King, well known personalities through their pilot training courses, share the spirit with Paul and Gail.

Aviation's small community is seen again as famed Australian adventurer Dick Smith and aviation icon Clay Lacy share moments of past escapades with Paul.

Dr. Bill Harrison and Dr. Michael Schloss greet test pilot great Scott Crossfield. In 1953, Crossfield was the first pilot to fly twice the speed of sound in the X-15.

GATHERING
OF ACES

In September, 2003, Gail and I were invited by friends Ed and Connie Bowlin to participate in a small gathering of Aces, who were getting together to sign lithos and share experiences. They all knew each other, and we were honored to be included in this historic event.

Jack Roush had just finished restoring his second P-51D Mustang and had arranged for me to shoot aerials of both planes.

Gail and I made lifelong friends that week and are proud to call these heroes and their spouses dear friends.

Wiley Sanders and his son talk over the history of his B-25 and the photo shoot that would take place in a few hours.

Ed Bowlin and Jay Wisner prepare for a flight.

Connie Bowlin knows a pilot's work is never done.

Jack Roush concentrates on his P-51s which are flying in formation with the B-25.

Paul usually shoots from the tail of the B-25, but sometimes he shoots through the open escape hatch.

Gail and Paul after a successful evening shoot.
Photo: Jack Roush

Jack and Paul are all smiles after an evening and sunset shoot of Jack's Mustangs.

Gen. David Lee "Tex" Hill and Gen. Robin Olds, who passed away June 14, 2007, of congestive heart failure

Miss Mazie and Tex

Tex admiring the Cub

Miss Mazie, Gail Bowen and Ellie Anderson

Gail and C.E. "Bud" Anderson

Paul, Gail, Connie and Ed Bowlin

Gail shot Bud Anderson and Gunther Rall as they shared some time of reflection. "Enemies" for years, they now enjoy a friendship and respect that only age and wisdom can bring together.

B-25 MITCHELL

Air-to-air photography is a very specialized type of shooting. It takes skilled pilots and photographers as well as the correct equipment. When you shoot aerials, the lead airplane is responsible for flying smoothly and not running into anything out there that would ruin your day – another plane, a tower, or "cumulo-granite." The plane that has formed up on the lead has the job of not hitting the lead plane. It sounds simple, but it's hard work. A great pilot with thousands of hours of flight time isn't necessarily a qualified formation pilot. It takes training and practice.

The best photo platform is the B-25 Mitchell bomber. Its cruise speed of around 170 knots is fast enough for any corporate jet to keep up with. With the tail cone removed, I can shoot the target in a variety of positions without having to shoot through glass. I have shot from 17 different B-25s, some of which have special noses, from where I can shoot when the planes change lead.

Owner: TallMantz Aviation

Owner: Aero Traders - *Pacific Princess*

Owner: The Air Museum Planes of Fame - *Photo Fanny*

Owner: Royal Netherlands AF Hist Flight - *Sarinah*

Owner: Russ Newman - *Old Glory*

Owner: Warbird Digest Magazine - *The Green Dragon*

Owner: American Air Power Heritage Foundation - *Devil Dog*

Owner: Larry Kelley - *Panchito*

Owner: Wiley Sanders - *Georgia Mae*

Owner: *Red Bull* - Innsbrook, Austria

Owner: Lone Star Flight Museum - *Special Delivery*

Owner: Jim Terry - *Pacific Prowler*

Owner: Wiley Sanders - *Ol Gray Mare*

Owners: Bob Lumbard & Bill Klaers - *In The Mood*

Owner: Tom Riley - *Killer 'B'*

Owner: Don George - *Axis Nightmare*

LEARJET DEMO TEAM & SAFETY STANDDOWN

"Godfather" Bob Agostino, director, Flight Operations, Bombardier Business Aircraft, created Bombardier's Safety Standdown in 1996. It is a "non-commercial effort to promote the philosophy of knowledge-based training and personal discipline." By bringing in expert speakers for seminars, workshops, and panel discussions, pilots can combine skill-based training with knowledge-based training.

Moderator Fred George, B/CA Senior Editor, addresses questions to esteemed panel participants Gene Cernan, R.A. "Bob" Hoover, Steve Nagel and Wally Schirra.

It's an annual opportunity to spend a few days meeting with other professional pilots who are also concerned with the issues of safety and bringing their professionalism to a higher level. Beyond the classroom, the informal opportunities to interact with contemporaries and share experiences make this such a popular event that hundreds are placed on the waiting list each year.

Bombardier does not charge a fee to the participants and invites pilots who fly non-Bombardier equipment. The Safety Standdown Team receives the support of the FAA and recently partnered with NBAA to provide this outstanding program.

Gail enjoys the company of friend and aviation icon Bob Hoover.

Bob Agostino escorts Paul and Gail into the Captain's Quarters a.k.a. the watering hole at the Hyatt.

Father Bill Johnson and son Dave Ryan enjoy their time together.

Nathalie Bloomfield of Bombardier Flexjet, and Gail surround astronaut Wally Schirra at the Standdown. Schirra passed away on May 3, 2007, of heart failure.

All the seasoned pilots love Gail, including friend and astronaut Gene Cernan.

Paul was honored by the Learjet Demonstration Team by being given a coveted Team jacket.

Paul's "brother" Bob Agostino, *The Godfather*, shares a proud moment as Paul, *Sharpshooter*, joins the Team.

Cessna Citation Special Olympics Airlift

Once in a while, we all do something we're proud of. Cessna and Citation operators can make all of general aviation proud with their Special Olympics Airlift. The 2006 Airlift involved 235 aircraft and crew participating in flying athletes to and from Des Moines International Airport for the Special Olympics National Games.

The Airlift Decals on the side of the Citation display the number of Airlifts in which this plane has been involved.

Russ Meyer helps an athlete de-plane as he excitedly heads for the games. For many athletes and coaches, this is their first time flying and certainly a first flight on a private jet.

Athlete Kenneth Hendricks displays his impressive collection of state pins. This return flight home was only the second flight in his life – the first being his flight out to the games.

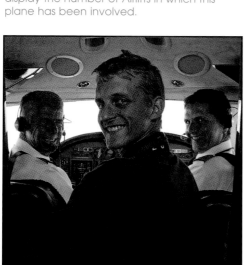

Athlete Bracey Absher turns for the camera and smiles at "The Photo Dude" as pilots Bill Wagner and Bob Dixon show him the front office.

The Medals tell the story, or at least part of it. Most athletes not only return home with medals and a sense of accomplishment, but return with new friendships.

Ed Parrish, Editor in Chief of Cessna Citation's *Directions Magazine*, tells athlete Laura Hays how proud he is of her.

Cessna's Chariman Emeritus Russ Meyer, Vice President of the Special Olympics Airlift Marilyn Richwine, and Cessna Chairman, President and CEO Jack Pelton and Jack's wife Rose

Cessna's VP of Marketing Phil Michel, *Flying Magazine's* Publisher Dick Koenig and Editor Tom Benenson, Russ Meyer, and Cessna's Senior VP Sales and Marketing Roger Whyte

GAMA President and CEO Pete Bunce, NBAA President and CEO Ed Bolen, and EAA President and CEO Tom Poberezney all share in the work and smiles of greeting arriving athletes.

Dove #1's crew poses with the boss. Left to right, Chief Pilot Bill Wagner, President Ted Townsend, and Pilot Scott Biller.

Ted Townsend, Bill Wagner and Marilyn Richwine congratulate athletes Melinda Simon and Laura Hays.

Flying Magazine's Publisher Dick Koenig, Cessna Vice President Communications Bob Stangarone, and Cessna Chairman, President, and CEO Jack Pelton enjoy a quick break.

Bracey Absher and friends show the world who's number one – they all three are!

Team Ohio shows the spirit of friendship and displays their team medals as they prepare to board a Citation for their flight home.

Athletes Kenneth Hendricks and Bracey Absher share a little North Carolina spirit on their return flight home from Des Moines.

Traveling home on Townsend Engineering's Citation X, one athlete displayed his medals and souvenier hat with friend's signatures.

Completing the journey: Coach Sandy McClinton, athlete Melinda Simon, Pilot Bob Dixon, athlete Bracey Absher, Chief Pilot Bill Wagner, athlete Kenneth Hendricks and athlete Laura Hays.

This says it all. The Cessna Citation Special Olympics Airlift allowed the athletes and coaches the opportunity to fly to the games in comfort and in speed.

NATIONAL BUSINESS AVIATION ASSN.

Paul's pal, NBAA Director Michael Herman, Paul, and CAN Executive Director Peter Fleiss meet at the CAN booth during NBAA 2006.

NBAA is *THE* organization for business aviation, and the annual fall NBAA Convention is *THE* event to attend. It's the opportunity for companies to introduce their new products, whether it be a new airplane or a new widget. It's also a great time to reunite with aviation friends.

Flying Magazine hosts an annual fundraising raffle for the Corporate Angel Network, with the winner receiving a free car lease. CAN is a charitable organization whose sole purpose is to arrange for free flights to treatment centers for cancer patients, using empty seats on corporate aircraft flying on routine business. I donate books each year, which are given to quantity raffle ticket purchasers. All proceeds are given to CAN.

Flying Magazine Vice President, Publisher Dick Koenig and M.B. Group Founder Jim Bernegger, work hard at public relations with booth staff, including *Flying* Marketing Director Maggi Finlayson.

Ashley Bowen Cook, Gail, and Sonia Greteman flash smiles at the annual NBAA Convention.

Patty Wagstaff enjoys a moment of celebration on her birthday.

Bill and Tish Fanning join Gail and Paul at the AVFUEL Corporation's annual NBAA Bash.

Business and Commercial Aviation Magazine's Executive Editor Jessica Salerno and *B/CA* Editor-in-Chief Bill Garvey, both long-term friends of Paul's share a break from the exhibit floor.

Saad Wallan, of Wallan Aviation in Riyadh, has become like a brother to Paul. A pilot, and owner of the largest car dealerships in Saudi Arabia, he also imports Cessnas into that region of the world.

Showing amazement that Paul actually owns a tie, and is in fact wearing one, are Learjet Demo Pilots, and Paul's buddies, Bill Landrum and Bob Agostino.

The aviation family is so small that you expect to see friends from all over the world. Gerard and Franciouse Pommier were visiting from Paris.

THE BRAZILIAN CONNECTION

I was on assignment for Cessna Citation in Brazil when I first met Comandante Rolim Adolfo Amaro in 1987.

Rolim loved flying, and he loved life. His passion for aviation took him from being a man of common means to the founder and CEO of TAM Airlines, the largest airline in Brazil. He also imported the Cessna product line into Brazil, which has the world's second largest fleet of Citation Jets, and he amassed a collection of 60 world-class vintage airplanes which has become the *Museu Asas De Um Sonho*. Sadly, Rolim was lost in a helicopter accident in 2001.

Rolim's wife Noemy, daughter Maria Claudia, and son Mauricio have carried on the business and become Gail's and my close friends. Rolim's protege, Rui Aquino, current President of TAM's general aviation business sector, has become like a brother to me. With Mauricio and Rui traveling regularly to Wichita, and Gail and me visiting Brazil frequently, we have shared fun times, and difficult times, and have grown into "extended family." In fact, Rui and Gail were born on the same day, and refer to each other as "twins."

Friends beget friends, so with more time in Brazil, came more friends. Special events in São Paulo meant Cessna was represented, and for Gail and me, friendships with Wichitans became enriched in Brazil. Roger Whyte, David Glassner, Mark Paolucci, Tracy Cassil, Todd Duhnke, and Texan Larry Cheek have shared more than a couple of caipirinhas in celebration.

The warmth of Brazilians is reflected in their eyes and can be summed up in this closing comment in a letter from Rolim to me, dated November 24, 1995 - "The longer you take to get here, the more I will be looking forward to seeing you again."

Mauricio, Noemy and Maria Claudia

Gail and Paul with Rui and Isabella Aquino

Rui and his daughter Leticia and son Filipe enjoy a meal at Fogo De Chao

Rui Aquino, Roger Whyte, Breno Correa, Tracy Cassil, Mark Paolucci, and Isabella Aquino

Paul and Gail, and Sonia and João Amaro

Gail, Noemy, and Paul

Neilton, Rui and Paul battle for Fashion King honors

Paul and Marco party late into the night. Sadly, Marco passed on in July, 2007. He will be missed!

Larry Cheek, David Glassner, and Roger Whyte from Cessna grab top fashion honors

Julio Banov Jr. and Joana (and João Henrique)

Jack Olcott and Rui plan the first LABACE traveling in a TAM Citation

Leticia and Felipe Aquino share smiles with their mother Marcia

EMBRAER

Embraer has been building regional jets for decades. Their reputation for quality craftsmanship and value have gained them a large market share throughout the world. Most recently, they've expanded their product line above and below the regionals.

Brazil is a large country, with land mass equal to that of the Continental United States, which gives me a lot of backgrounds to choose from when shooting aerials. I've had the fun of flying low over the beautiful Brazilian coastline, past mountains and lakes. But the most fun was flying low over the Amazon in a C-130 with three planes in tow. With two video shooters along and cameras in everyone elses hands, we directed most of the Brazilian Air Force into an aerial ballet. Great food, great views, and great adventures with great friends. And I get paid, too?

Directors Dalila Andrade and Regiane Marchesini are now good friends. When you get up early in the morning and work late into the night for days on end, you develop life-long friendships. Plus, I appreciate their patience as they have tried to help me learn Portuguese. *Obrigado!*

BOOKS, POSTERS, CALENDARS, NOTE CARDS, FINE-ART WALL PRINTS AND STOCK PHOTOS

In addition to the warbirds in this book, our product line showcases breathtaking images of corporate jets, piston singles and twins, propjets, sport planes, helicopters and more. Our collection includes a variety of posters, notecards, original photographs, calendars and books. The 24" x 30" lithographed posters and 5" x 7" fold-over note cards are established favorites. Our books, *Air To Air, Volumes I and II*, and *Volume III - Warbirds*, excite a wide range of readers beyond aviation enthusiasts and make great gifts. In 2002, we introduced our first oversized wall calendar. Pilots especially enjoy the wide variety of 11" x 14" original photographs, and are a popular choice for home and office decor. You may call Paul's studio at 1-800-697-2580 or visit our web site at **www.airtoair.net**.

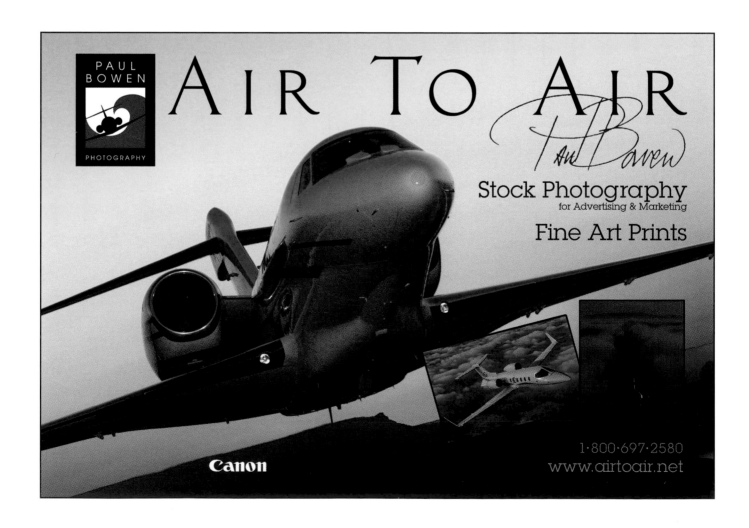

OUTTAKES

1. Pat and Betty Rowley are Paul's mentors. Paul owes his career to Pat and Betty.
2. Musicians Scott and Pamela Brownlee were Paul's friends from California in the 60s. They currently own the Rockin' B Ranch Cowboy Dinner Theatre in Liberty Lake, Washington. Joining them at Prairie Rose are Paul and Gail's close friends, Drs. Rick and Kim Hartwell.
3. A gaggle of friends gather at the water, at the Bowens, for a July 4th celebration.
4. Jimmy Yarnell has been a photographic and advertising inspiration to Paul for decades. An admired photographer, Jimmy was head of advertising at Beech when Paul first began his career in the early 1970s.
5. Robert Arnold, grandson of Gen. Hap Arnold, from Chandelle Winery, and Alan Cannon and K.R. Rombauer of Rombauer Vineyards in St. Helena, California, donated refreshments to a Doolittle Raider's Reunion at Travis Air Force Museum.
6. In the catacombs with Koerner Rombauer, Paul's extended family enjoys a personal tour of the caves that help make Koerner's wine so famous. Koerner is a great friend, a longtime pilot currently flying his own CitationJet, who has a great passion for warbirds and the freedoms they have brought us.
7. Gabby and Aubrey Winters enjoy Christmas cookie making with Auntie Gail.
8. Paul's been surfing since around 1959. Here he strikes a pose at Puamana, in 2006.
9. Cessna test pilot Mort Brown, one of Paul's pilot heroes, celebrates his 99th birthday in July, 2007.
10. Bob "OLE" Olsen, master custom surfboard craftsman and surfing legend, shares a moment in his Maui shop with Paul's brother Lance.
11A. David Glassner shares a dance with Noemy Amaro in Brazil.
11B. Paul and Mark Paolucci share drinks at Yia Yias.
11C. Gail at Tanya Johnson's farewell party before Tanya moved to Atlanta.
11D. Marcelo Moreira and Amanda Heraclio adjust to Kansas winters.
12. Lee Lauderback and Angela West enjoy the Tetons while hiking with Paul and Gail.
13. Daughter Ashley Bowen Cook's friends Mali Thompson, Megan Redmond, and Heather Dillon, celebrate Ellie Flower Katz' wedding.
14. Hot Times in the Bowen's Tub. Young friends gathered to welcome Leticia Aquino on her first visit to Kansas from Brazil: Dylan and Evan Senn, Maggie, Kaylee and Suzanne Cocke, Megan Munson, Sarah Pritchard, Brandon Harrouff, Lindsay MacAdam, Kyle Taylor, Scott Siemens, Leticia Aquino, Alisha Emond, Nick Anneler, Josh Lipscomb, Josh Reeves and Laura Hunter.
15. Hats just seem to work better with Gail than with Paul.

1

2

3

4

5

6

7

8

9

10

11A

11B

11C

11D

12

13

14

15

Outtakes

1. Paul, Jim Koepnick, Russ Munson, and EAA Sun 'n Fun President John Burton take a break from the annual fly-in at Lakeland, Florida.
2. Paul and Gail join Ralph, Nancy and daughter Katherine Aceti in New York.
3. The Ya Ya's GNO group have been evading the local police for two decades.
4. The International Society of Aviation Photographers group meets annually to share knowledge and friendship. Fellowshipping over sushi are Dave Carlson, Russell Munson, Dean Siracusa, Dave Metz, Tom Jenkins, Paul, Gail and Chad Slattery.
5. The Hawaiian Mafia at East of Java in Honolulu, includes Bruce Lagareta, Gail, Suilan Ellsworth, Paul, Wendy Lagareta and Michiko Sukai Smart, Saburo Sukai's daughter.
6. The Air Museum Planes of Fame in Chino, California, is where many of Paul's warbird friends are based. Enjoying the tradition of Rosa's Italian Cuisine, are Lisa Collinsworth, John Dramesi, John Hinton, Karen and Steve Hinton, Brent Hunter (deceased), A.J. Schad, Kevin and Andrea Eldridge, and young Steve Hinton.
7. Another ISAP group – Standing: John Dibbs, Mark Wagner, Caroline Sheen, Pam Dibbs, Claes Axstal, Gail Bowen, George Kounis, Tyson Rininger, and Ross Koty. Kneeling: Arnold Greenwell, Russ Munson, Paul, Jim Wilson, and Michael Pliskin.
8. The Salt Company was a singing group in the sixties based out of the First Presbyterian Church of Hollywood. Paul was deeply involved with their ministry to the street people. Paul and Gail joined the group in 2004 for a concert tour through California. Pictured are groupies Paul and Gail, Chad Gallion, David and Sharon Covington, Pamela Van Valin Brownlee, and Deborah and Bob Marlowe. Brian Hahn, original Salt Company bass player, died in 2003.
9. Prairie Rose Cowboy Dinner Theatre is a fun spot near Wichita to entertain international guests. This evening, our friends from Cessna included: Mark Paolucci, Roger and Ingrid Whyte, Ursula Jarvis, Saad Wallan, Gail, Trevor Esling, Marilyn and Ed Parrish, and Annie Roebuck.
10. This was an incredible visit with our friend Miguel Candia in Paraguay. Gail and I started our first evening with a sunset tour of the local lake, champagne on his boat dock while being serenaded by native folk music on a harp, followed by a fantastic barbeque and fun time meeting new friends. The next day we went to their flying club and shot aerials. Gail took this picture of Rubén Bruyn, Edgar Insfran, Paul, Roberto "Beto" Vierci, and Miguel in front of the Fleet.
11. Paul belonged to a club at North Hollywood High School, the *Jesters*. This annual group photo was taken around 1964, with Paul "surfing" the water ski. These *Jesters* were: Mike Grimes, Marty Goldhaber, Greg Rast, Joel Hickman, Pat Laughlin, Charles Ruble, Bill Rakow, Don Reid, Cliff Holt, Bob Reid, Mike Dobrich, John Mason, Terry "Ace" Duarte, Rick Edmisten, Pete Arnold, Paul Ranslow, Pete Van Trite, Ken Paine and Paul.
12. In February, 2004, the *Jesters* had a reunion. Before the official event began, a few of us stopped by Bob's Big Boy Drive In, in Toluca Lake, for a taste of memories: Dr. Paul Ranslow, Charles Ruble, Pat Laughlin, Donn Carper, Craig Fergus, Lt. Col. John Teele, Rick Edmisten, Bob Archer, and Paul.

1

2

4

3

Ya Ya's
girls nite out

Marla   Anita   Gail   Debbie   Lana   Cristi   Kristi

5

6

7

8

9

10

11

12

Outtakes

1. Deanna Harms, Tamara Cook, Nancy Blanchat and Sonia Greteman join the party for Paul's 60th, April 6, 2007.
2. Daughter Aubree greets Brad, Tammy and Keenan Cox.
3. Evan, Ashley, and Dylan join in on the Big Kahuna's celebration. Paul and Gail's close friends Bruce and Wendy Lagareta sent Paul the fresh orchid lei from their home in Honolulu.
4. Aubree and Paul after a Beechcraft photo shoot.
5. Gary and Christina Warden share an NBAA moment with Paul and Gail.
6. Gail and Paul, and Marilyn and Ed Parrish – gettin' wild at the movies.
7. Carol and Don Hoch, and daughter Tamara and husband Corky Cook, congregate around son Jake at Paul's party. Jake's brother Josh is married to Ashley Bowen Cook.
8. Chloe celebrated her 12th in February, 2006.
9. The Augusta Ya Yas gather around Dylan the Cabana Boy: Ruth Lawlor, Kristy Schrag, Gail, Susan Pangrac and Lori Primm.
10. Not to be outdone by Chloe, Paul strikes the pose for his 60th birthday invitation.
11. David Glassner and Paul pose outside David Paul's Lahaina Grill.
12. David's Brazilian Angels: Andreia Andrade, Livia Theodoro and Fernanda Cardim.
13. Mark Paolucci and Karyn Page are groupies for the night, at a fund raiser "battle of the bands." Cessna's band entry, named *Don't Know Jack*, refers to Cessna chairman, president, CEO, and all-around good guy, Jack J. Pelton.
14. Siblings Tico, Marcelo and Mariana Moreira from Brazil, join Santa.
15. Close friend and NASCAR legend Jack Roush hosts Paul and Gail and two of their four children, Dylan Senn and Ashley Bowen Cook, at the Kansas Speedway in October, 2005, for their first NASCAR race. Being the ultimate host, Jack "arranged" for his five teams to place first, second, third, fifth and 17th, with Mark Martin taking the checkered flag.
16. Don and Pat Hysko prepare the sangria for Paul's 60th party.

1

2

3

4

5

6

7

8

9

10

11

12

13

14

15

16

Outtakes

1. Magic Man Ed Parrish earns his dinner performing for Jack Roush, Brenda Strickland and Connie Bowlin.
2. Chuck Hosmer and Paul were Senior Class presidents at North Hollywood High School, in 1965. Paul was winter class president and Chuck was summer. Chuck attended the Air Force Academy and recently retired as a Captain with American Airlines. Summer 2005 found them at their 40th class reunion.
3. The Arnold girls were Sunday School students of Gail's and Paul's years ago. They are now wonderful ladies with children of their own: Megan Gardner, Becky Timberlake, and Karen Cantu.
4. Dave Ryan tries on the latest in Learjet Demo Pilot wardrobe.
5. Aubrey and Roberta Hastings, friends of Paul's and Gail's, are maternal grandparents of Paul's two daughters, Ashley and Aubree.
6. "Tip" shows off the latest design. Paul and Gail always enjoy Tip's company when they visit Maui. Check out Maggie Coulombe Designer Dresses, 505 Front Street, Lahaina, Maui.
7. Kecia and Justin Ladner surround chef Jeremy Wade from Uptown Bistro in Wichita. Gail and Paul enjoyed their most fantastic meal, prepared by Jeremy, and served to 12 lucky people at Justin and Kecia's.
8. Paul and Mark Paolucci during a birthday board meeting in Kansas City.
9. Gotta have breakfast somewhere. Might as well be at 35,000 feet in a Lear 60. Ashley Bowen Cook, husband Josh, and parents Corky and Tamara Cook joined Gail and Paul for a flight to visit friends at Korbel and Rombauer.
10. Ashley, Tamara and Gail - Wine Chicks
11. HUXLEY Bandmembers Derek Alley, Evan Senn (Gail's son), Scott Siemens, and Trever Lockamy.
12. The staff at Hope Community Church shows they are there to SERVE. Paul and Gail attend this fellowship, but unfortunately, this is not their car.
13. Avery and Addison pick on Uncle Paul.
14. Charlie and Gayle Johnson know how to enjoy life. Charlie, past president of Cessna, is currently working in Colorado with Javelin. Gayle, previously an advertising executive in Wichita, now has her hands full with Charlie's Colorado Adventures.
15. A great fishing day in Maui with Dylan, Aubree, Nathan, Janelle, Matthew and Janae.

1

2

3

4

5

6

7

8

9

10

11

12

13

14

15

OUTTAKES

1. The Bowen Bunch 2004: Josh (Kansas State University) and Ashley Cook (University of Kansas), Evan Senn (Wichita State University), Aubree (University of Kansas), Dylan Senn (Kansas State University), Gail (Ozark Bible College), Paul (University of California at Santa Barbara) and Chloé (Obedience School Dropout).
2. Cora Bowen, a.k.a. MOM, celebrates her 85th at Mama's Fish House on Maui in 2005, with sons Lance and Paul and brides Catherine and Gail.
3. Don and Imogene Hilton, Gail's parents.
4. Lance, Paul and Corky Cook after a morning surf session.
5. Margie and John Block have been friends of Paul's since the late 60s. John and Paul were involved in a church in Hollywood and roomed together for a while. Guess who got the big bed? Retired from playing for the NBA and coaching college ball, John now runs an inner-city gym ministry, The Lord's Gym in San Diego, and is setting up an Olympic basketball program in the African country of Benin.
6. Sister Sisters, Ashley and Aubree were both Kappa Kappa Gammas at KU. Aubree pursued her drama interests during her later college years.
7. Ashley with Jaime and Bryan Easum, good friends of the Bowen Bunch.
8. Don and Imogene Hilton, Gail's parents, celebrated their 50th anniversary in 2004, and are pictured here with their 16 grandchildren and spouses, and one great-grandchild.
9. Abe and Casy Stuever Dreiling.
10. Dylan with "cousins" Alex and Weston Kloefkorn.
11. Nate and Cady Stuever Tibbs.
12. Dylan and Evan.
13. Ashley and Gail enjoy themselves at a fundraiser.
14. In spring of 2007, Aubree played the lead roll at KU in *Lily Plants a Garden*.

1

2

3

4

5

6

7

8

9

10

11

12

13

14

Acknowledgments

Some people who have not been mentioned, or briefly mentioned, have made contributions to this book or to my life. This is my opportunity to say, "Thank you."

My family and friends are very important to me. Most of my family still lives in California, including my mother, Cora Bowen, my Aunt Milda Gibbons, Uncle Paul and Aunt Marilyn Myers, and "The Third Bowen Brother," Dr. Steve Johnson, wife Fran, and three adult children.

Hawaii has become another home to me, along with southern California where I was raised, and the Wichita area where I've lived since 1971. My Hawaii connections are especially strong with my only brother Lance and wife Catherine living on Maui. Lance is an incredibly talented graphic designer, specializing in cartooning, and pastors Nu 'Oli (Glad Tidings) Community Church in Lahaina. Hawaii houses high school friends transplanted from North Hollywood, Bruce and Wendy Lagareta, and Roland and Kitty Lagareta. More Hawaii friends include Gary and T.J. Cia, Renaldo, Jennifer, Summer and Ocean Macedo, and Amy Cabingas and Margo Gill at Puamana. My surfing buddies include Lance, Al Nip, Kim Ball, Jonathan Wu, and Andrew Gallagher. I'm in awe of the surfing skills of Tom Hughes, Gary, Greg, Terry, Randy, John, Dave, Mike, Eric and Michelle, Fritz, and Randall. Sadly, on July 3, 2007, we lost James "Moon" Enoka Kauhane – a great surfer and soul.

Many of our friends are involved in aviation. Some are clients, some are suppliers, and so many of them are friends. Ralph and Nancy Aceti continue to be favorite companions of Gail's and mine. Al Higdon, Dick Koenig, David Charney, Steve Fushelberger, and Jim Swickard and Jessica Salerno, are well known within the aviation community. We work closely with Jon Potts and Hal Shevers at Sporty's Pilot Shop. We also supply our books to John and Martha King for the King Catalog. We've enjoyed dinner in San Diego with them and our close friend "Uncle Fred" George – as our kids call him. Paul, Audrey, Tom and Sharon Poberezny have contributed so much to aviation and are truly nice people.

Kansas is now my home and it's filled with strong friendships like Tom and Jan West, Wayne and Norma Roberts, Michael Phipps, Sheri Dierking, David, Rhonda and Austin Mann, Phil and Carina Michel, George and Elizabeth Charlsen, Mike and Jan Hahn, Dick Yauk, Cheryl Cordry, and Ed and Marilyn Parrish. Other Kansas friends include, Pete and Ruth Lawlor, Tammy and Brad Cox, Jim and Rita Bunck, Brett, Bridget and Cletus Kappelman, Becci Hargrove, Mike and Paige Cocke, Kent and Janet Kruske, Bryan and Jamie Easum and Earlene Condiff. Pam Winters and Bill O'Connor keep us in shape at APEX, while Jay and Beth Tully tempt us at Cocoa Dolce Artisan Chocolates in Wichita.

Manned flight has come a very long way since Kitty Hawk. With the Centennial Celebration in 2003 of the Wright's first flight, we realize how quickly we have advanced in aviation. Certainly World War II produced a huge number of new designs and technological leaps that have helped bring us to our current level. Interestingly enough, these warbirds were built half-way into the history of aviation and yet today they still fly with power and grace.

Our other international friends include Federico "Freddy" and Olly Wenzelmann, and Eduardo Whaite from Venezuela. The Kajese family is spread out around three continents. Parents Sam and Rose live in Harare, Zimbabwe. Son Mutsa, currently resides in Zim. Son Farayi lives in the U.S.A. on the east coast and daughter Vimbayi lives in Beijing. Farayi, Vimbayi and Mutsa are all graduated from the University of Kansas.

I'm proud to be sponsored by Canon, having been included in Canon's elite group of professionals, The Explorers of Light. Thanks to Dave Metz, Steve Inglima, Dave Carlson, Fred Metzler, Brian Matsumoto, Steve Losi – and Eddie Tapp, friend and Photoshop Guru.

The International Society of Aviation Photography is a great group. Started in 2001 by Jay Miller and Chad Slattery, an annual convention features speakers and a "shooting field trip." I serve on the board with some wonderfully talented people who have become close friends. The ISAP Board and the entire aviation community lost a truly talented photographer and a fine man on April 20, 2006, when George Hall died. He and the others we have recently lost will be remembered.

A final thanks to Pastor Steve Weldon, who keeps Gail and me fed on a regular basis at Hope Community Church in Andover, Kansas.